YOU CAN RIDE

If you want to learn to ride and take care of a pony then this is the book for you.

As an aid to your proper riding lessons you will find all the information and advice you need to know to tack up, mount, trot, canter and take your first steps towards jumping; and the correct way to groom your pony and take care of your riding equipment. The history of riding, useful organisations to contact, tournaments and riding events – these, too, are fully explored and explained in this essential handbook for new riders.

Other titles in the YOU CAN series include:

YOU CAN PLAY FOOTBALL with Gordon Banks
YOU CAN BE A GYMNAST with Avril Lennox
YOU CAN SWIM with David Haller
YOU CAN PLAY CRICKET with Ted Dexter

All published by CAROUSEL BOOKS

YOU CAN RIDE

A CAROUSEL BOOK 0 552 54232 6

First published in Great Britain by Carousel Books

PRINTING HISTORY
Carousel edition published 1983

Carousel Books are published by
Transworld Publishers Ltd.,
Century House, 61–63 Uxbridge Road,
Ealing, London W5 5SA

Made and printed in Great Britain by the
Guernsey Press Co. Ltd., Guernsey, Channel Islands.

You Can Ride

with Joan Davies

Illustrated by Mike Miller

CAROUSEL BOOKS
A DIVISION OF TRANSWORLD PUBLISHERS LTD.

CONTENTS

	Page
A WORD FROM JOAN DAVIES...	7
A WORD OF WARNING	9
THE HORSE	11
THE HISTORY OF RIDING	12
WHAT IS A PONY?	16
RIDING CLOTHES AND WHEN TO WEAR THEM	18
APPROACH	21
CATCHING	21
LEADING	22
LYING UP	23
PICKING OUT FEET	25
GROOMING	28
Grooming kit	29
How to groom	30
PREPARING TO TACK UP	34
TACKING UP	35
The bridle	35
Snaffle	37
The saddle	38
Parts of the saddle	39
MOUNTING	41
Mount in four stages	42
DISMOUNTING	46
Common faults in dismounting	47
POSITION – or how to sit on a pony	48
AIDS TO WALK FORWARD	50
Halting	51
HOW A PONY MOVES	54
Walk	54
Trot	56
Canter	58
The rein back	59
HOW TO TROT	60
The sitting trot	60
The rising trot	60
Diagonals	62
HOW TO CANTER	65
FIRST STEPS TO JUMPING	68

FALLING OFF 70
RIDING IN COMPANY 72
RIDING ON THE ROADS 74
THE COUNTRY LORE 80
SIGNS THAT A PONY NEEDS SHOEING 81
CLEANING TACK 83
OWNING A PONY 90
  The type of pony 90
  What a pony will need 91
HOW TO LOOK AFTER:-
  The field 98
  Tack 100
  Grooming kit 101
  Rugs 102
LOOKING AFTER YOUR PONY DURING THE SEASONS 104
  Spring 104
  Summer 105
  Autumn 106
  Winter 106
FEEDING 109
HANGING UP A HAYNET 111
GENERAL CARE 113
COMPETITIONS AND ORGANISATIONS 114
HUNTER TRIALS 116
TEAM CHASING 117
POINT-TO-POINTS 118
SHOW JUMPING 120
DRESSAGE 124
LONG DISTANCE RIDING 127
EVENTING 131
POLO 134
CAREERS WITH HORSES 138
FAMOUS RIDERS 142
USEFUL ADDRESSES 149

A WORD FROM JOAN DAVIES . . .

My own interest in riding began when I was a child. Like most young riders, I worked my way up through Pony Club, gymkhanas and general hacking, which finally led me to long-distance riding. We used to go on day-long rides, which later in life led me to Post Trekking, a form of riding in which you move from one site to another each day, carrying all your clothes and equipment in saddle bags.

After I had done two long treks on my own, I took four children with me on my next one and found that they learned a great deal about riding during our holiday on horseback. This type of riding appealed to me in particular because of the need to train both horse and rider to a great degree of fitness.

In 1969, I watched my first Golden Horseshoe Ride and realized that there was far more to this sport than met the eye. I saw that there was a great need to study it carefully, especially with the importance of teaching riders the correct method of training. I then bought my first pure-bred Arab, Zarpa. He won three gold awards in Golden Horsehoe rides and did, I believe, the fastest time over 75 miles, 9.67 m.p.h.

Few people are lucky enough to find a second lifetime partner, but my beloved Kossak Lad has certainly proved to be a very special person. I hope that you will find an equine friend that you can care for and share many happy hours in each others company.

Joan P Davies

A WORD OF WARNING

This book does not set out to teach you to ride without attending proper lessons. It is written to try to help you understand what you are learning and to teach you, step by step, the correct way to approach and look after a pony.

If I can give you two pieces of advice from my experience, they are these. Never take risks and **always** think what you are doing. And, accidents can happen, but if you take care, they will not be serious ones.

Now read on and enjoy yourself. Happy riding!

P.S. Always wear a hard hat when you ride.

THE HORSE

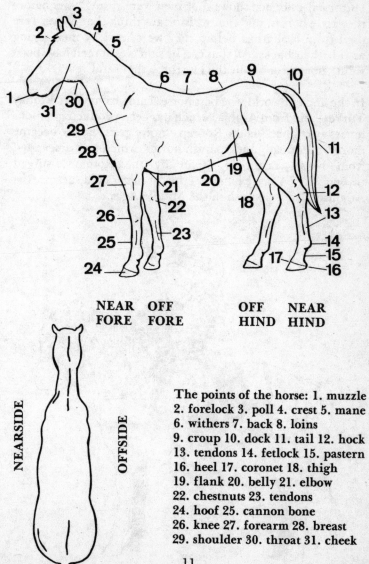

NEAR FORE   OFF FORE

OFF HIND   NEAR HIND

NEARSIDE

OFFSIDE

The points of the horse: 1. muzzle
2. forelock 3. poll 4. crest 5. mane
6. withers 7. back 8. loins
9. croup 10. dock 11. tail 12. hock
13. tendons 14. fetlock 15. pastern
16. heel 17. coronet 18. thigh
19. flank 20. belly 21. elbow
22. chestnuts 23. tendons
24. hoof 25. cannon bone
26. knee 27. forearm 28. breast
29. shoulder 30. throat 31. cheek

11

THE HISTORY OF RIDING

No one knows for certain when men started to ride horses. Historical evidence shows that men were riding asses before they rode horses, and many historians think that horses were used to pull chariots before they were used by men sitting astride their backs. All that can be said is that men have been riding horses for about the last three thousand years.

In the ancient world, the best horses came from what is today Turkey, and from Arabia, which has been producing famous horses ever since. As the Roman empire grew, horses became more widespread, and Spanish horses, which had descended from horses taken to Spain by the Romans, spread throughout America, after they were taken across the Atlantic by the Spanish in the Middle Ages.

Horses have been used as a means of transport, they have been used in warfare and they have been used in sport. Today, the first two uses have almost disappeared, but the sporting horse is probably more widespread and popular than it has ever been. Although the military connection with riding is now restricted to ceremonial occasions, most riding sports owe their development to military training in the past, and there are still many fine riders in the world's armies. One of the most famous is Captain Mark Philips, who is no longer serving in the British army, but who rose to fame in the riding world while he was an army officer. Twenty years earlier, two Italian brothers, Piero and Raimondo D'Inzeo, became equally famous in the riding world and both of them were cavalry officers.

Many equestrian sports (sports involving horses, from the Latin word *equus* − a horse) have changed in the twentieth century, but old sports like **hunting** and **polo** are much the same as they have always been. In the case of polo, which is described later, some of the rules have been altered, but the game is largely the same as that played by Persian princes hundreds of years ago, when it first appeared.

Hunting itself gave rise to sports like cross-country riding and steeplechasing, which developed from friendly races held between two very fast horses to decide which was the faster. This also led to professional **horse racing** as more and more attention was paid to the breeding of horses, so that they would be able to run faster and faster.

Today, we think of world famous horse races like the Derby, the Kentucky Derby, the Grand National and the Prix de L'Arc de Triomphe, but in the twelfth century St. Thomas Becket described a horse race in which he called the riders 'jockeys' and two hundred years later, the Prince of Wales, later King Richard II, challenged the Earl of Arundel to a race between their two fastest horses. This shows that horse racing for prize money is a very old sport, and also shows why racing became known as 'the sport of kings'.

The sport of **dressage** really began when the first man sat on the back of a horse and made the horse go where he wanted. After all, the purpose of dressage is to train a horse to move as the rider wishes. The Greek general and writer, Xenophon, wrote books on riding four hundred years before Christ was born and his books were used as the basis for the sport when Italian riders began to train their horses in what is called the 'classical style', in the fifteenth century. The exercises became more complicated and demanding as training methods developed and great schools of riding were founded to train both riders and horses in very detailed, perfectly controlled moves. Some of these schools still exist. One of them is the **Spanish Riding School** at Vienna, famous for its Lipizzaner horses. The exercises they perform date back to seventeenth and eighteenth century riding masters.

Eventing, one of the most popular equestrian sports today, has its roots in ancient Greece too. Xenophon was careful to train his horses and their riders so that they could cope with every riding condition they were likely to meet. He wanted them to be fast and to have great reserves of stamina as well. The result was a training programme that we would recognise as an event. Throughout history, other cavalry leaders followed his example. Between the seventeenth century and the beginning of the nineteenth century, **long distance riding** was an important part of cavalry training. The rides varied between less than 50km to over 400km, but they all had the same purpose, to train the horses to cover long distances and to train the riders to look after them on the ride.

Endurance riding was linked to jumping and dressage for the first time by the French cavalry. In 1902 they held an exercise, the **Championnat du Cheval d'Armes**, which was the forerunner of the modern event. Each horse had to compete in a dressage test, an endurance ride, a steeplechase and finally a show jumping competition. Since then, eventing has become increasingly popular. In 1924, the Olympic event was opened to civilian riders and since the early 1950's civilian riders have dominated.

British riders took less interest in eventing than riders on the continent until after the Second World War. Then, in 1949, the Duke of Beaufort held a three-day event at his home at Badminton in Gloucestershire. This was intended to be part of a series from which the next British Olympic team would be picked. The event proved to be such a success that the **Badminton Horse Trials**, as it is called, has been held ever since. Today it is one of the leading competitions in the world.

Show jumping is a comparatively recent sport as well. The Royal Dublin Society held a contest for 'high' and 'wide' leaps at their show in 1865 and this is believed to have been one of the very first show jumping competitions, though it was nothing like the colourful, nerve-racking competitions we are used to watching today. Show jumping started in Russia and France at about the same time, and by the end of the nineteenth century there were competitions at most agricultural shows in Britain. Show jumping featured in the **Olympic Games** in 1900, but it was not until 1912 that equestrian sports became regular Olympic competitions.

As with eventing, army officers dominated show jumping until thirty years ago. In 1948, all 44 competitors in the show jumping competition at the Olympic Games were serving in cavalry regiments. Since then, more and more civilians have reached the top and the greatest rise to success has been among women riders. For in riding, men and women are equally matched, and in recent years in particular, it has been the women who have frequently come out on top.

WHAT IS A PONY?

A pony is a four-legged person who becomes more human as you get to know each other.

A pony is not a machine which will go all day.

A pony needs food, water and rest.

Ponies come in all shapes, sizes and colours and have very varied temperaments.

Ninety-nine ponies out of a hundred really enjoy being ridden.

There is an old saying:

'*One end bites,*

And the middle is uncomfortable to sit on'

The first two lines can certainly be true if the pony has been badly treated or teased. The third line is only true until you have mastered the Art of **Sitting on** and **Riding** the pony.

RIDING CLOTHES AND WHEN TO WEAR THEM

When you are riding informally in warm weather, a short-sleeved shirt, jodhpurs and jodhpur boots or long boots are the most suitable clothes. You must **always** wear a well-fitting hard hat, preferably with a flexible brim. You should have a cord under your chin to make sure that the hat stays on — particularly if you are going to ride on a road.

The correct way to wear a riding hat is well forward not on the back of the head.

If you are going for a riding lesson you should add a jacket and put on a tie and gloves.

When you are riding in cold weather, you'll probably find a polo-neck jumper and jacket the best clothes to wear. If you're riding in a field, you might prefer to wear an anorak instead of a jacket.

Your boots should always be clean and polished and you should look neat and tidy yourself.

Girls should wear their long hair in plaits, a pony tail, or in a net. **Never ride with you hair loose**. This can be very dangerous if it blows in your eyes and prevents you from seeing where you are going. It also looks very untidy.

APPROACH

Ponies are very sensitive. They will try to run away if they are frightened and as they can hear very well, you will upset them if you shout or run up to them.

When you go to catch a pony in a field, always take something with which to catch him. **A carrot sliced lengthways or an apple cut in quarters** will be very acceptable. If ponies were supposed to eat sweets or sugar, someone would have invented a toothbrush for their teeth by now. No one has invented a toothbrush for ponies because they should not eat these titbits. They are very bad for them.

It's important not to carry anything in your pockets, either, as this encourages a pony to search you and snap at you if he cannot have what he wants.

CATCHING

Approach a pony from the front, holding out your apple or carrot, and keeping the headcollar behind your back.

Call to him so that he knows you're coming. He will often walk towards you. Put the rope round his neck and give him the apple or carrot. Now put on the headcollar by putting it over his nose and flicking the headpiece over, so that it can be done up on the near-side.

LEADING

It is safer to lead a pony with the correct equipment, not with just a rope a round his neck, since it gives you greater control.

Before you set off, wait for him to finish his mouthful and then walk briskly beside his shoulder.

TYING UP

The first step in tying up a pony is to make sure that there is **a small loop of binder twine** fixed to your stable ring or on the rails, if you have to tie him outside. **This is very important.** If the pony pulls back for any reason, he will break the twine and not his headcollar. There is also another advantage of using a loop of twine. If you cannot untie the **quick-release knot** because the pony has pulled it too tight, you can cut the twine and replace it later with a new piece.

Tie the pony using the knot shown. You can untie it quickly by pulling on the loose end of the rope.

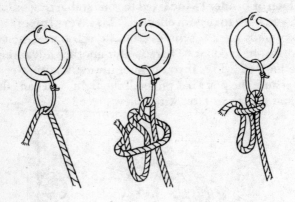

When you tie your pony, make sure that you give him enough rope to let him feel comfortable, but not so much that he can stretch his head to the ground or get a leg over the rope.

If you are going to ride him, he must not be given a hay net, but if you are only grooming him, he may have a small net to keep him happy.

See **How to tie a hay net**, page III.

PICKING OUT FEET

You will need a **bowl** or a **skep** as well as a **hoofpick** when you go to pick out a pony's feet, since you do not want stones and mud left in his stable or on the yard. Before you start picking out his feet, pick up any droppings lying around him, otherwise he will fill his feet up again when he walks about.

Begin by placing the bowl just behind the pony's left front leg. Face **backwards** (towards his tail) on the **near side** and run your **left** hand down the **back** of his near leg.

Hoof pick

Pick up the long hair at the fetlock joint and say *'up'*. Hold the toe of the hoof with your right hand and cup your left hand round the hoof to support it. Holding the hoofpick in your right hand, start from the **heel** and clean down to the toe of the hoof, being careful of the frog, which is the sensitive part in the middle of the foot.

Repeat on the other side of the frog. Clean the **cleft** of the frog very gently.

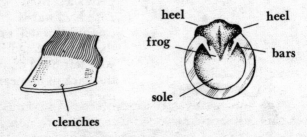

clenches

heel

heel

frog

bars

sole

All the dirt should now have fallen out into the bowl, so pick this up before putting down the pony's foot. Take a few steps forward, place the bowl behind the pony's nearhind leg.

Run your **left** hand down the **front** of his hind leg, and round the **back** of his fetlock, to pick up the long hair or the joint itself. Say 'up' and repeat the procedure as for the front leg.

Now go **underneath his neck** — never round the back of the pony. Place the bowl behind the right front leg. With your

right hand, run down the back of the front leg as before. Use your **left** hand to hold the toe while you cup the hoof with the right hand. This time use the hoofpick in your left hand, though if you are very right-handed, you can hold the hoof with your left hand and clean with your right.

Clean the offhind foot as you did the nearhind foot and remember to run your hand down the front of the hind legs — never the back. If the pony kicks out, at a fly for example, you can drop the leg without being hurt. But if your arm is **behind** the kicking leg, you may be injured.

Once you have picked out all the pony's feet, empty the bowl and put the hoofpick into it. Put it away.

Now is the time to oil the pony's hooves, if they are free from mud and are dry. Oiling acts as a protection and keeps the horn in good condition.

While you are picking out the pony's feet, you should also check that his shoes are safe and are not worn out. A **lost shoe** means that he cannot be ridden on the road. A **loose shoe** means that he cannot be ridden at all until he has been seen by a blacksmith.

By feeling round the outside of the pony's hooves, you can find out whether there are any *'risen clenches'*. This means that the nails used to attach the shoe have worn almost through the shoes and the pony needs to visit the blacksmith.

If there are 'risen clenches', you will be able to see the nails sticking out of the hoof. This is dangerous as the pony may cut himself on the sharp nails.

GROOMING

Reasons for grooming:

1. To remove mud, sweat and general dirt.

2. To clean the coat.

3. To tone up the skin and thoroughly clean it, so that the pony can sweat more easily.

4. To tone up the muscles.

5. To make sure we inspect all the important places and keep his coat in good condition.

6. To make him look smart.

Grooming Kit	Uses
Dandy brush **Plastic curry comb**	To remove caked mud and loose hair in spring
Body brush (The bristles are softer and shorter than those of the Dandy brush)	To remove grease and dust from the skin and coat. To brush the mane and tail.

Metal curry comb	To clean the body brush and **NOT** the pony.
Water brush	To 'lay' or flatten the mane and make it lie on the correct side **(offside)**. You can also use a separate one to wash the hooves.
2 sponges (different colours if possible)	One for eyes and nostrils. One for dock
Stable rubber or chamois	This is used to polish the coat.
Small bucket of water	To damp the sponges. **NEVER** use the drinking water.

GROOMING KIT

Dandy brush

Plastic curry comb

Body brush

Metal curry comb

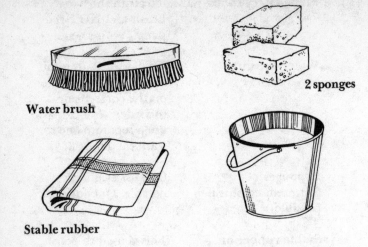

Water brush

2 sponges

Stable rubber

How to groom

You will find it easier to groom your pony if you can do it under cover. If you have to groom him outside, **tie him facing into the wind**, not backing into it. This way round, the dust you brush out of his coat will not blow back onto the clean area.

1. Start by picking out his feet as described.

2. Using the dandy brush or the plastic curry comb, remove all the mud from his coat on both sides.

3. Gently brush his face **using the body brush only.**

4. Now brush his mane with the same brush, cleaning right to the roots which will be scruffy and greasy. **Do not lay the mane at this stage** as you may get his body wet.

5. Take the body brush in your **left** hand and the metal curry comb in your **right**. Go to the near side of the pony and, facing his tail, use short circular strokes to clean the coat and skin thoroughly. **Clean the brush with the metal curry comb every 4-5 strokes**. Draw the brush carefully through the comb and tap out the dirt on the floor. Work from neck to tail thoroughly cleaning the wither and elbow areas.

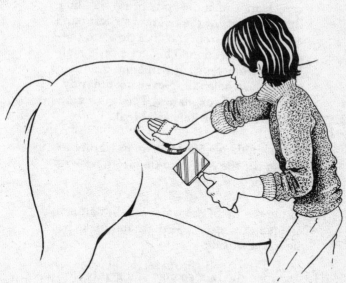

6. Go round to the front of the pony. Put the body brush in your **right** hand and the metal curry comb in your **left**. Brush under the mane and all over the body. Clean the brush thoroughly. Put the curry comb down in the grooming box. Brush the legs carefully with the **body brush**, being careful not to knock any of the bony places.

7. Clean the body brush and put it away.

8. Now go to the tail. Take out all the knots and twists in the hair using your fingers and make sure that it is completely free from mud. Once you've done this, you can clean it with the body brush, holding the main part of the tail in your **left** hand and brushing from the dock down to the end of each section. Then let a little more hair go from your left hand and gradually brush the whole tail. **Never use a dandy brush on tails or manes**. The bristles are too hard and the hair will break.

9. Use a stable rubber or chamois leather to polish the the coat, working from neck to tail as before.

10. Using the tip of the water brush, dampen the mane — do not **soak** it, and make it lie to the offside.

11. Dampen the **face sponge** and gently clean the corner of the pony's eyes. Rinse the sponge. Now clean both his nostrils. Clean the sponge thoroughly and put it aside to dry.

12. Take the **dock sponge**, dampen it and clean under the tail. Wash this thoroughly and put it aside to dry.

13. Put all your equipment back into the bag or box and put this away. Check that you have not left anything lying around.

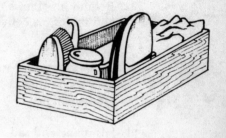

PREPARING TO TACK UP

1. Pick out the pony's feet and check his shoes.

2. If the pony is clean, check:

    a. Behind his ears

    b. Behind his elbows and under his belly

    c. In front of his withers and the area where the saddle will lie.

    d His mane and tail.

3. **Make sure that he has had nothing to eat for at least one hour.**

4. Make sure that you are neat and tidy and correctly dressed.

5. Now collect your saddle and bridle.

If the pony is in a stable, you can put on his bridle first, so that you have control of him. To begin with, put your tack in a safe place.

Untie the rope and take off his headcollar — **do not take off his headcollar while he is tied up**. He may pull back while you are unbuckling it and frighten himself. Put the headcollar outside the door, or hang it up.

TACKING UP

The bridle

Ask someone to help you, if you are not experienced.

Stand on the nearside, facing in the same direction as the pony. Put the reins over his head. Keep your **right** shoulder against his **left** one. Put your right arm under his neck and hold the cheek pieces together, in front of his face, with the bit just below his mouth.

Put your **left** thumb into the corner of his lips where there are no teeth. He will open his mouth. Raise your right hand up his face and gently slip the bit into his mouth. Keep the bridle straight by lifting it up his face, so that the bit stays in his mouth.

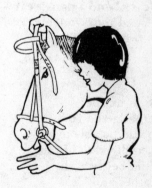

Now put your **left** hand on the headpiece at the very top. Still keeping your right hand under his neck, put your fingers behind his **right** ear and prick it, by gently pressing it forward. Slip the right side of the headpiece over that ear. Now bring your right hand back under his neck and prick his **left** ear. Slip this one under the headpiece. Straighten his mane and forelock.

Never bend a pony's ear – you wouldn't like it if somebody treated yours roughly. Ponies can be made difficult to bridle by rough handling.

Draw up the throatlatch. You should be able to get the full width of your hand between the leather and his cheekbone.

Draw up the noseband, allowing two fingers between the leather and the pony's face.

If you have a curb chain, take hold of the last link. Twist it to the **right** until it is completely flat. Now place the bottom of the **last** link over the hook. Tighten it by putting the second link over the hook. When fitted correctly, the chain should lie at an angle of 45° away from the chin groove.

SNAFFLE

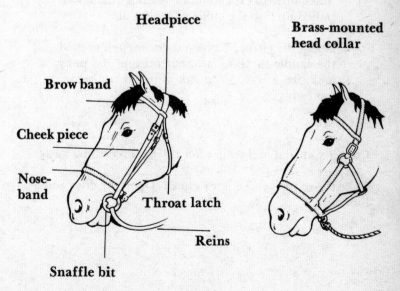

Headpiece

Brass-mounted head collar

Brow band

Cheek piece

Nose-band

Throat latch

Reins

Snaffle bit

The saddle

Make sure that that there is nothing under the numnah before you place it on the withers.

Always make sure you have attached the numnah and girths to the saddle before you leave the tack room, and check that the girths are over the seat.

Place the saddle on the withers and slide backwards until it sits comfortably in the correct place.

Go round and put the girths down. Never throw them over the saddle. They may hang crooked or bang against the pony's joints.

Make sure that the numnah is straight and well pulled up into the gullet of the saddle.

Do up the girths. Tighten them enough to hold the saddle in place, without making the pony look like a wasp. You can adjust them before mounting.

Collect your hat and whip after tidying everything away.

Take the reins over the pony's head. Open the door and lead him out.

PARTS OF THE SADDLE

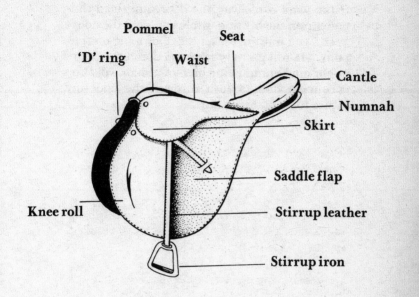

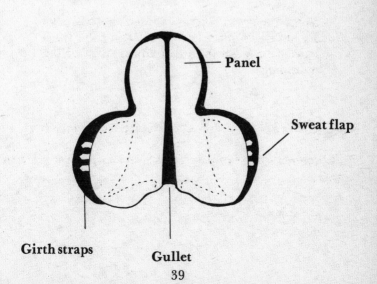

39

IMPORTANT

If the wind is blowing the door shut, lead the pony from the **off** side, while you hold the door open. You must never let the door bang on the pony. He will get very frightened and the door might injure him. Being hit by the door will also encourage him to rush through the door in future to avoid being hurt.

MOUNTING

When you are ready to mount, adjust your girths, run down your stirrups and check that they are the correct length. To do this pick up the stirrup in your left hand and, putting the fingers of your right hand up to the stirrup bar, put the stirrup into your right arm pit. If it reaches comfortably, it is about the correct length. Some people have longer arms than others, and you may find that putting your knuckles against the stirrup bar gives you a better guide.

Now make sure that the pony is standing on level ground and standing **'square'**. This means he has 'a leg at each corner', like a table, and not one front leg well in front of the other. If he is standing incorrectly, when he feels your weight in the stirrup, he will have to move, in order to balance himself. You will then be left hopping around on one foot, or worse still, will sit heavily in the saddle, as you get thrown off balance.

Let's assume that the pony is standing correctly, these are the stages you must go through to mount him properly:

Stand on the near side facing his tail.

Take up the reins and whip in your *left* hand.

Mount in four stages

1. *(a)* With your right hand, take the back of the stirrup iron and turn it outwards, towards you. *(b)* Gently put your **left** foot into it, pointing your toe downwards, so that it will lie under the pony's belly and not poke into him. Now, using your right hand, hold the front or **pommel** of the saddle.

2. Spring up, straightening your left knee and putting your heels together. Stand very upright and do not lean over the saddle. You should now be looking directly over the saddle. PAUSE.

3. Swing your right leg over the back of the saddle, keeping it straight, at the same time turning to face the front, and sit down gently in the saddle, with your right knee touching the saddle before your seat does.

4. Without looking down, turn your right toe inwards towards the girth and pick up the stirrup. Take up the reins in both hands.

The pony must stand still while you do all this. If you have a fidgety pony, ask someone to hold him and your right stirrup while you mount. If he is always made to stand square, without moving, you will find mounting very easy.

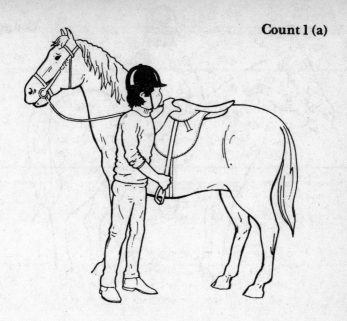

Count 1 (a)

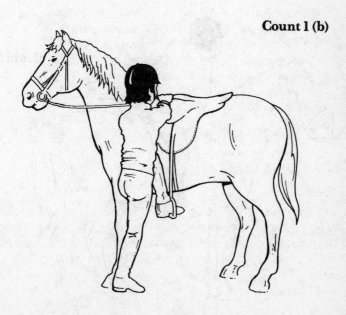

Count 1 (b)

Count 2

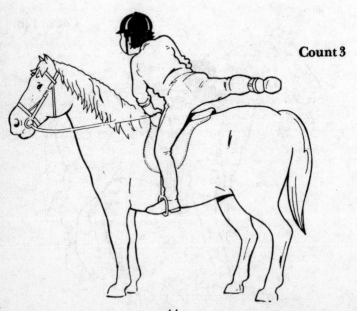

Count 3

44

When you are completely ready and have checked your girths, you can ask him to move forward. He must go forwards before he is asked to turn. **Never ask a pony to turn while he is standing still.**

DISMOUNTING

1. Make sure your pony is on level ground and 'standing square'.

2. Put both reins and your whip in your **left** hand and hold the pommel, making sure that your right rein is slightly longer than the left. Until you are good at dismounting, you could pull the reins as you reach the ground, if your left hand slips.

3. Take both feet out of the stirrups.

4. Swing your right leg clear of the back of the saddle, **keeping it straight.**

5. Pause with both heels together and leaning over the saddle.

6. Drop quietly to the ground, bending your knees and keeping your feet together.

   Put your reins over the pony's head and run up your stirrups.

Common faults in dismounting

1. **Allowing your right leg to be bent as you swing over the back of the saddle.** This means that you can get your right foot caught up on the cantle and you may fall over as you land badly.

2. **Keeping the left foot in the stirrup.** If the pony moves off, you could be left hopping along after it.

3. **Failing to pause,** while leaning over the saddle will result in an untidy drop to the ground and may mean that you sit on the ground through being unbalanced.

4. **Pulling the pony's mouth with the right rein if it has not been left longer than the left rein.** If you let go of the pommel as you drop to the ground, your right rein will be pulled sharply over to the nearside of the pony.

5. **Failing to make the pony stand still.**

6. **Holding on to the saddle for support as you drop to the ground.** This may pull the saddle over with you and bruise the pony's withers.

POSITION – or how to sit on a pony

Sit in the middle of the saddle.

Let your legs hang down either side. If your feet are out of the stirrups the bottom of the stirrup should touch your ankle bone. The leather should hang straight down, not being pushed forwards when your foot is in the iron.

Sit tall, with your shoulders straight and your neck 'feeling' the back of your collar. Now make your head sit properly on your neck – without it tipping to one side. Some riders look like robins looking at worms on the ground!

You should be able to
hold a long stick
vertical to the ground,
with it passing by your
ear, shoulders, hips
and heel.

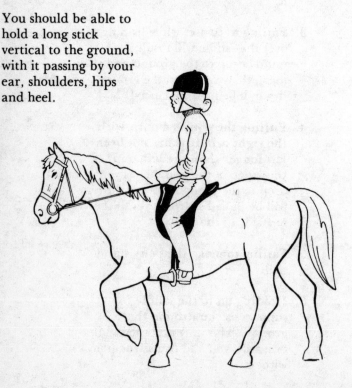

Pick up your reins and hold them with the little fingers downwards and the thumb on top. You can pretend that you have a mug of your favourite drink in each and you must not spill a drop of it!

The correct way to hold the reins can be described like this. Pretend that you have a tiny chick in each hand. If you hold it too tightly, you will squeeze it to death. If you have a loose, 'open' hand, the chick will fly away.

Bend your elbows so that the top part of your arm lies beside your body.

Be sure your reins are of equal length and that your pony is not asked to walk with his head to one side.

49

AIDS TO WALK FORWARD

Sit tall, but be ready to go forward with the pony. If you are not ready, you will be thrown off balance, your hands will come up and you will jerk his mouth.

Squeeze the pony's sides firmly with both legs at the same time, as though he was a big Brazil nut and your legs were the nutcrackers. Release the pressure as he moves forward.

A pony moves away from the leg that is pressing hardest against him. So:-

If you want to go **right**, keep your right leg still and press him hard with your **left** leg. With your hands, indicate by turning your right thumb in the direction in which you want to go. Therefore, to go **right**, use your **left leg** and **right thumb** — to go **left**, use your **right** leg and **left** thumb.

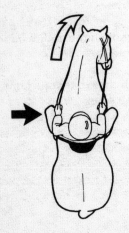 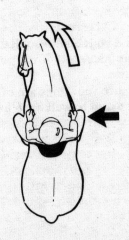

Don't forget to straighten the pony up or he will go round in circles.

A well schooled, obedient, pony will move forward with firm leg aids. If he is 'hard of hearing' and pretends that he doesn't understand, use firmer pressure, or transfer both reins to one hand and tap him smartly with your whip, just behind your leg. He will soon understand that if he does not obey the leg first time, it will hurt later on!

Allow yourself to relax as he is moving forwards, keeping him straight, and look up in the direction in which you are going. If you are always looking at the saddle or down at the ground, you will be altering your weight in the saddle. What's more you will fail to notice any obstacles in your path, or the traffic coming towards you.

Halting

When you want to halt, you have three sets of brakes. Your **seat** and **legs** stop the back part of the pony, where his 'engine' is. The third set, the **reins**, should only be used in emergencies, or if the pony has not understood your leg/seat brakes.

Riding a pony is similar to riding a bicycle downhill. You know what happens if you only apply your front brakes on a bicycle — the front wheel stops, the back wheel carries on and you fly over the handlebars. Something rather similar happens with the pony. If you fail to stop the back part, it still carries on, pushing the front part along. This causes the pony to screw round, because his back part can't go in the correct direction.

If you sit deep and squeeze equally with both legs, keeping your back nice and straight, keeping your hands still and not allowing the pony's head to go backwards and forwards, he will come to gentle halt, because he is being asked to with all three sets of brakes.

Reins are not there to **pull** ponies around. They are there to ask tactfully, once the engine, or driving force has been given its instructions. Always **think** what you are asking your pony to do and you will not make mistakes. It is enough, provided you have the reins the correct length, to 'feel' them. There is no need to **pull** them.

Keep your heels down at all times, especially when you are asking for a halt. If you have your heels up, you are more likely to dig them into the pony's sides, which gives him the instruction to GO ON!

Keep your knees on the saddle and your toes pointing forwards.

This will help you tread evenly in both stirrups. If you put more weight on one stirrup, you unbalance yourself and your pony. It also means that you cannot give him the correct instructions.

You may use your voice quietly, but don't 'cluck' at the pony with your tongue. You are not a mother hen calling her chicks and this is a lazy way of making a pony go.

HOW A PONY MOVES

One of the most important points you can learn when you start to ride is how a pony moves under you. As you become more experienced, you can feel each leg moving, but, to give you a basic idea, this is how he moves his legs in a walk, a trot and a canter.

Walk

This a pace of **4 time**. Each hoof goes down separately:

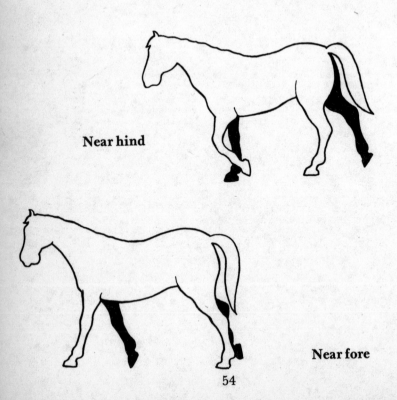

Near hind

Near fore

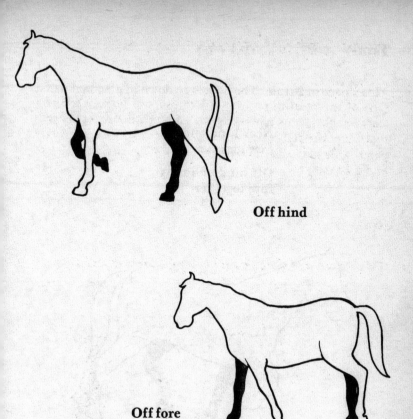

Off hind

Off fore

You hear four hoof beats on the road and the pony's head moves slightly up and down.

Trot

This a pace of **2 time**. The hooves go down in diagonal pairs:

Near hind and off fore together

Off hind and near fore together

You hear only two hoof beats on the road and the pony's head should be absolutely steady unless for some reason he is lame.

If you have difficulty in seeing how the trotting legs move, ask someone to bandage the pony's near hind and off fore legs, leaving the other diagonal legs unbandaged. When he trots, you will be able to see how the bandaged legs work together.

Canter

This is a pace of **3 time**. You can hear three beats clearly if the fields are hard. **NEVER canter on the road.**

The pony is said to be cantering left when he is going in a left-handed circle and his **near fore** is leading in front of his **off fore**. The order of hoof beats in the left-handed canter is:

Off hind

Near hind/Off fore together

Near fore

This gives the three beats, since the **right diagonal** (near hind and off fore) go down together.

The near fore, the fourth leg to go down, is called the **'leading' leg** because it is the one that strikes new ground in front of the others. If the pony is going round to the left, he must **lead** with this leg, or he may slip on the corners and come down. This could happen as he would have to cross his front legs in an effort to get round the bend. A very well-schooled pony may have less of a problem as he and his rider will be better balanced.

You can easily see which leg your pony is leading on; if you glance down at his shoulder on the inside of the circle. This one should be going further forward than the outside shoulder.

For a right-handed circle — **canter right**:

> **Near hind**
>
> **Off hind/Near fore**
>
> **Off fore**

go down in that order — the off fore being the 'leading leg'.

The rein back

This should not be tried on a young pony as he is not mature or balanced enough to do it correctly. You will need to know exactly what to do before you ask for a rein back — walking backwards. This is certainly not a matter of 'pulling the pony's mouth' until he steps back.

The correct sequence of events as the pony goes back in diagonal pairs is:

> **Near hind/Off fore**
> **together**, then
>
> **Off hind/Near fore**
> **together**

This is an advanced movement and you **must** be shown how to do it.

HOW TO TROT

There are two types of trot — the **sitting trot** and the **rising trot**.

The sitting trot

In this trot you sit quietly in the saddle, with your seat still and your legs well down either side of your pony. Your heels should be pointing down and you should **not** grip the saddle.

Inexperienced riders often fall into the common fault of bringing up their knees, in an effort to grip the saddle. They imagine that by gripping, they will stay on the pony! Nothing could be further from the truth. If you bring your legs up the saddle, you are much more likely to fall off. Watch a Red Indian sitting on his horse in a western film. He sits very proud and tall. His hands are quiet. His legs are long and hang right down the side of his horse. The only time he falls off is when he has an arrow in his back.

So, when you are sitting to the trot, think of the Red Indian — though you are unlikely to have arrows flying around.

The rising trot

As the name suggests, in the rising trot you spend some time out of the saddle, in fact you spend half the time in the saddle and half the time out of it. While you are sitting to the trot, you should be able to 'feel' the thrust from the pony's quarters, which is trying to throw you up out of the saddle. When you feel this, try putting more weight in the stirrups

and rising just out of the saddle. You should never rise so high that your knees are straight. This will jar you when you get to the top of the rise and will make you miss the next beat as you spent too long in the air! If you just come out of the saddle each time, it will be easier to sit gently back into it and will give the pony an easier time.

It will take a lot of practice before you can rise evenly every time. Once you think that you've really got it right, practise **sitting** to the trot going round corners and when changing direction, and rising to the trot when you are going straight. A pony finds it a greater effort going round a bend and will tend to slow down. If you are sitting in the saddle one hundred per cent of the time while he is making this turn, you can push him forward with your seat. It will also make you keep your legs in the right position if you really have to think about what you are doing.

Diagonals

A pony trots at a pace of 2 time, which means that diagonal pairs of legs go down together. When you are going round corners or riding circles, it is important to help the pony as much as possible. I have said that it is a greater effort for a pony to circle and go round corners than to travel in a straight line. Watch a pony performing these manouevres and you will see that his inside hind leg is placed much further underneath him when turning, than when going on the straight.

> To help him, you must be sitting in the saddle when **that leg** is on the ground. You should be rising out of the saddle as the leg is lifted up and placed forward. Obviously you can't look behind and underneath a pony while he is trotting – so look instead at the pair to that diagonal – the **outside front leg.**

> If you rise out of the saddle as the outside front shoulder/leg goes forward, you will be sitting as it comes to the ground. Since these legs work together, you must also be sitting as the **inside hind leg** is on the ground.

Now, as you trot round **glance**, don't lean forward, and look at that outside shoulder. Is it swinging forward as you swing up out of the saddle? If you are not sure, look at the **inside shoulder**. What is that one doing? If it is going forward as you **rise** – then you are sitting on the wrong diagonal leg. To change to sitting on the correct diagonal leg, all you need to do is **sit one extra bump**. Changing the diagonal is a matter of following this rhythm:

Up Down Up Down **Down** Up Down Up Down

It's easy when you understand.

When you have to change the rein and are going the other way round, during school manouevres, you must be sure that you are **'on the correct diagonal'**.

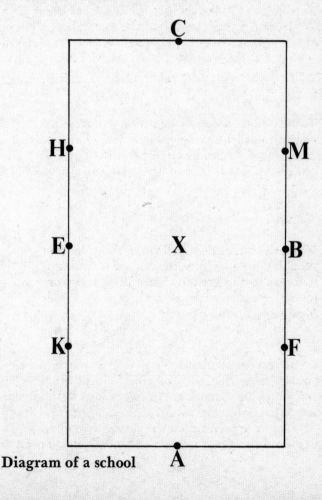

Diagram of a school

As you go through the centres of the school, called 'X', you should do one extra bump, so that you will be on the correct diagonal when you reach the next bend.

HOW TO CANTER

As I've said earlier, the canter is a pace of 3 time.

I've mentioned also how the horse 'strikes off' with one hind leg, followed by the opposite diagonal pair, with the 'leading foreleg' last. It is important to understand this, and whenever possible, you should watch a pony moving so that you know what is happening:

You need to do three things to ask a pony to canter. It is **not** a question of kicking him until he canters. This only produces a fast, unbalanced trot.

> You should not attempt to canter until you have done work without stirrups, and are secure in the saddle. You should also be riding a safe, schooled pony when you canter for the first time, and this should take place in an enclosed area, not in a field.

The change from a trot to a canter involves asking the pony to switch from a pace of 2 beats to one of 3 beats, which produces a totally different feeling. To achieve this change, you need to sit to the trot to steady and strengthen the pony's stride so that he will be able to 'spring' into the canter when you ask him.

You need to have good 'contact' with his mouth, which means having him under control without pulling at him. You also want him to turn his head slightly to the inside, so that he will lead with the correct inside leg. How do you do this?

Sit deep in the saddle.

65

'Feel' the inside rein so that he turns his head slightly.

As you approach the corner, bring your **outside** leg back firmly to just behind the girth and press the pony hard.

You must sit up and not lean forward. At first you might find it easier to hold the front of the saddle by putting two fingers under the arch and pulling yourself slightly into the saddle. Keep your weight in the stirrups to stop yourself bouncing.

The pony must be well under control, so that he alters his pace to a canter and does not trot faster and faster. To sum up, the aids to canter are:

Sit to the trot

Feel the inside rein

Keep the inside leg still, bring the outside one back and press hard.

This should cause the pony to strike off with the outside hind leg, followed by the opposite diagonal and the inside front leg last of all.

While you are cantering, sit quietly to the 'rocking' movement, keeping a steady rhythm going at the corners.

When you want to return to a trot, follow this sequence:

Sit deep in the saddle

Keep your legs and heels down

Squeeze firmly with both legs and

Keep sitting to the trot

Once the pony has settled into a steady trot, you can rise.

FIRST STEPS TO JUMPING

Before you start jumping over small fences, you must be completely safe trotting and cantering. If you start to jump too soon, you will pick up bad habits and may spoil the pony because you jab his mouth.

The very first stage in learning to jump is going over ground poles, carefully spaced, so that you become expert at placing the pony and having the correct position when the pony steps over the poles. You can have one raised slightly off the ground to give the feeling of what it is like when the pony gives a little leap.

The golden rule of jumping is never look down or back at your jump — however small it is. **Always** lean forward, looking through the pony's ears.

Give him enough rein to stretch his neck over the jump and lean your body slightly foward to 'go with him'.

Watch other good riders jumping so that you can see what the pony does and what the rider does.

Remember — make haste slowly. You get better results that way!

FALLING OFF

Nobody likes taking a tumble, but it does happen occasionally and it is a very good idea to know how to fall. Here are some Do's and Dont's:

Do

1. **Always wear correct protective clothing.** There is nothing clever about riding without a hard hat, or riding in plimsoles.

2. **Relax and curl into a ball.**

3. **Let go of your reins,** unless you land on your feet and can control yourself and the pony quickly.

4. **Stay where you are on the ground,** so that other ponies won't tread on you. A pony will always jump someone lying on the

70

ground. He will not try to kick you or
stamp on you.

5. **Check you tack BEFORE remounting.**

6. **Reassure your pony.** He may be upset by
what has happened, and it probably wasn't
his fault anyway.

Don't

1. **Don't try to hold on to your pony** – you
can get dragged.

2. **Don't jump up as soon as you fall off.**
You may be winded and it is better to sit
still for a moment.

3. **Don't run after your pony.** You may
frighten him and make him get his feet
caught in the reins. Go quietly to him.

4. **Don't punish your pony.** He won't
understand what he did wrong.

RIDING IN COMPANY

There will come a time when you are safe enough to ride out with others. To do this, you must be sure that your pony is good in company and won't be a nuisance. Always remember that through careless riding you put others in danger.

Be courteous and considerate. Don't crowd at narrow places or gateways.

Keep a safe distance from another pony and don't risk treading on his heels. A correct distance should allow you to see the bottom of the tail of the pony in front of you.

Chatting to another rider may prevent you from paying attention to your pony or the traffic around you.

Make sure that you and your pony always appear neat and tidy. It is rude to arrive with a dirty pony and dirty tack. Always check that your boots are clean, too.

Carry a hoofpick in your pocket. You might not need it, but there may be someone else who does.

Watch out for other riders when you are cantering in a field. They may not be as safe as you are and by dashing past, you may cause them to have an accident.

If somebody falls off, stop your pony immediately and warn the other riders. The loose pony will also stop, and somebody can catch it. If the rider is hurt, dismount and either give your pony to someone else, and go to the injured rider, or see that someone else does. If you can avoid it, do not lead a pony to an injured rider. You won't be of any help like this and there is always the risk that your pony might accidentally step on the person on the ground.

If a rider is really hurt, leave him or her lying on the ground and, if you can, wrap him or her in a jacket. Send one of the others to fetch help, but **on no account** try to move the injured rider.

Always leave someone with an injured rider, even if the other riders go home for help.

RIDING ON THE ROADS

Always wear correct protective clothing.

Make sure that your tack is safe and that your girths are tight enough.

If your pony is traffic shy, don't venture out without a traffic proof pony to accompany you. Keep this pony on the **traffic side of you.**

Whenever possible, keep to grass verges and do not ride on main roads with heavy traffic.

Motorists do not realize how slowly ponies move or that they can be frightened by things moving in the hedge.

You must know what road signs and signals mean, and you must obey them.

Always ride on the left-hand side of the road and ride in single file.

Here are the hand signals that you must give:

I intend to move out
or turn to my right

Please STOP

STOP

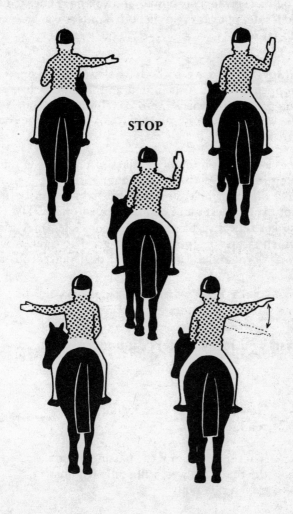

I intend to pull in
or turn to my left

I intend to slow down
or stop

Always give motorists plenty of warning before manoeuvring.

Once you have given your signal, and you have checked that the road is safe, put your reins in both hands as you have more control that way.

Always thank drivers who have slowed down or stopped for you. A deep nod and a smile is all you need give if you want to keep both hands on the reins.

If there is a risk that it might get dark or foggy while you are out riding, take **reflecting equipment** with you − either a vest, or a diagonal belt, or armband, which can be fitted easily into your pocket and can be slipped on quickly. (You can also get reflective bands for the pony's legs). A stirrup light which straps on to your leg is good too and a white headscarf worn under your hat will also make you more visible.

Motorists and lorry drivers do not realise:-

How fast a pony can shy out into a road.

That spray from a car passing when the roads are wet, will really frighten even a safe pony.

That a pony may shy if he sees something in a hedge.

That if a high-sided vehicle brushes the side of a hedge, this will frighten a pony more than it would if it passed close to him.

That plastic bags flapping on roofracks are very frightening.

Danger areas for you to remember and watch for

1. Parked cars can have dogs sleeping in them which may jump up and bark as you pass them.

2. Lawn mowers used in gardens or by the road can frighten ponies.

3. Hoses or garden sprinklers will certainly frighten a pony when they are in use.

4. Children kicking balls about. You should **halt** until the ball has stopped moving.

5. Skate-boards and their riders are another hazard.

6. Balloons at fêtes can cause trouble.

7. Field guns going off at regular intervals can be very noisy.

If you are leading a pony . . .

On foot

1. Always wear a hard hat.

2. Always lead with a bridle − never a headcollar.

3. Walk on the traffic side of the pony and on the left-hand side of the road.

4. Make sure you have your stirrups run up correctly.

From another pony

1. Make sure that all the tack is safe.

2. Lead the pony on the **left**, keeping your pony on the traffic side. (You have more control of your own pony as you are sitting on it).

3. If the unridden pony is saddled, make sure that the stirrups are really secure.

The stirrup leather is put through the iron as usual, and is then bent forward and back through the iron. The free end can be passed through the loop of the leather and then put through the side keeper. This makes sure that the iron does not slip down the leather and knock against the pony, which would certainly frighten him.

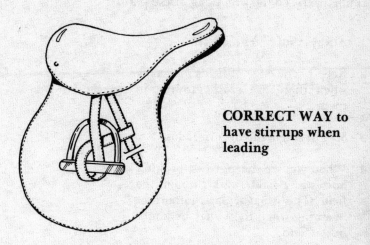

CORRECT WAY to have stirrups when leading

THE COUNTRY LORE

There are certain rules that you must observe when you are riding in the country or along bridle paths:

1. Always shut gates securely.

2. Keep to the edge of fields especially when there are crops growing in them.

3. Stay in single file in corn fields.

4. When you see sheep, cows, or other horses in a field, **walk** through the field. This is particularly important in spring when there may be lambs in the field.

5. If you see an animal in distress, try to find the farmer who can come and help it.

6. Give way to walkers, they may be nervous of horses.

SIGNS THAT A PONY NEEDS SHOEING

A pony will need to be reshod every 4-6 weeks, depending on how much road work you are doing and the rate of growth of his hooves.

Danger signs:

A lost shoe

Shoes that are loose

Risen clenches — the ends of the nails that are keeping the shoe in place are sticking up around the outside of the hoof.

A shoe which has twisted inwards so that one branch is sticking into the pony's frog.

The hoof splitting and growing out over the shoe — if the pony has been left for too long before being reshod.

A 'tinny' sound when the shoe comes to the ground, instead of the usual 'ring'. This means that the nails have broken off inside the hoof and the shoe will come off if you go through mud, as there is nothing to secure the shoe to the foot. Accustom yourself to the normal sound of the pony's shoes on a road. If you hear anything unusual, dismount and look at the shoe.

Watch your farrier when he shoes the pony. He may put on a new set of shoes, or he may put on the old set again, when he has re-shaped them. This is called **Removing**. It doesn't mean taking them off altogether!

You should check every shoe whenever you pick out your pony's feet.

CLEANING TACK

Points to remember – Why do we clean it?

The three enemies of leather are:

1. **Heat** – leaving leather by a fire or heater to dry will dry it too fast and will make it crack.

2. **Water** – getting leather soaked and leaving it wet.

3. **Neglect** – not looking after leather and allowing mildew to form on it, or leaving it lying about to be trodden on.

Danger areas to watch every time you use leather

1. Wherever metal touches leather, it makes a black mark. Places to watch for are where the bit touches the cheekpieces and the reins and where buckles are joined to other pieces of leather.

2. Holes in leather weaken it, so it is important to alter the cheek pieces by putting one side up a hole and the other side down a hole. This 'spreads' the wear, while still keeping the correct fit.

3. Stitching can also wear. Always check that it is safe. Particularly on stirrup leathers.

Leather has two sides. The outside is called the **grain side** and has been waterproofed. The inside is called the **flesh side** and has not been treated. It is rougher and collects all the grease and dirt from the pony. This is the side you must be particularly careful to clean as it becomes dry and brittle.

To clean tack, this is what you need:

2 buckets of warm water

1 sponge or cloth to soap the leather

½ bar or tin of saddle soap

An apron for yourself

Metal polish and a cloth

Towels

This is what you do:

Bridle

1. Wipe away any mud from the leather with a sponge or cloth.

2. Make a note of the holes on which your buckles are positioned − then you will be able to put the bridle together again without difficulty.

3. Lay out one towel to receive the cleaned leather.

4. Take off the bit and put it in one bucket. Put this to one side so that it does not get soapy.

5. Undo the bridle and put the pieces ready to be cleaned.

6. Start with the **headpiece**. Using a damp sponge, rub on the soap and thoroughly clean the leather. Rinse your sponge often, you will be surprised how dirty it becomes. Be sure to wring it out thoroughly. You must not get the leather too wet and you will find that it gets frothy if your sponge is too wet as well.

7. Clean the browband next, putting each piece on the towel.

8. You can fit the browband onto the headpiece now, especially if there are lots of you cleaning tack together and you may get your pieces mixed up.

9. The cheek pieces come next. Thoroughly clean the places where the bit has touched. Check the stitching. Put them on the headpiece.

10. Clean the noseband.

11. Clean the reins. Do not put too much soap on these, or you will not be able to hold them on a wet day.

12. Wash the bit. Dry it thoroughly and if you wish, polish the parts that **do not** go in the pony's mouth.

13. Put the bit and reins on the bridle and link the reins through the throat latch. Hang the bridle up with the browband and noseband facing outwards. Be careful not to use too much soap, or you will make the leather sticky.

14. Dry the bridle with a towel, do not hang it near a fire, or heater.

Note

When you put a snaffle bit onto a bridle, be careful to put it together carefully. You should be able to get the two rings close together when it is on the bridle. If you cannot do this, turn them until they shut together and then put the bit on the leather. If the bridle is put together incorrectly, it will pinch the pony's tongue.

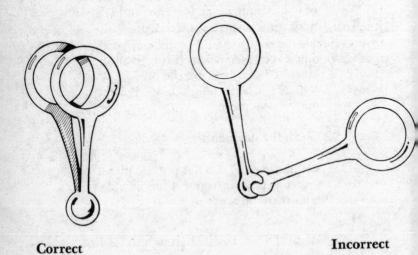

Correct   Incorrect

If you have a curb bit, make sure that the port, or raised part for the pony's tongue to pass under, is upwards. The curb chain remains attached to the offside, at all times but must always be removed from the near side hook before tacking up and untacking.

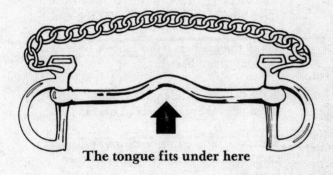

The tongue fits under here

Fastenings

Remember that **stud fastenings** should be done up on the **inside**. Buckle fastenings should be done up on the outside so that they don't scratch the pony's face.

The saddle

1. Make sure that your water is clean.

2. Take the leather and irons off, and put the stirrup irons into a clean bucket of water. You can scrub the treads, if you have any, and replace them at the end.

3. Hang the leathers from a hook. It is easier to clean them like this.

4. Take off the buckle guards and clean them. Put them on a clean towel.

5. Turn the saddle upside down and put it carefully on a blanket to protect the leather.

6. Clean the lining with soap, if it is leather, and with a brush if it is not.

7. Clean the whole of the saddle − under the flap and the outside as well. Where the stirrup leather comes down the flap, you will find grease and dirt collects. You will find it much easier to remove this if you put your hand under the flap and 'push' the dirty leather upwards. This will open the groove enough to allow you to clean out the dirt.

8. A little Neatsfoot oil will help keep the leather soft, but this must only be applied to the **flesh side**. Do not oil the grain side, as this has been waterproofed and the oil will stay on the top and will not

soak in. It will make your jodhpurs dirty if you oil the top of the saddle.

9. Put the buckle guards and stirrup leathers back on the saddle and lift it onto a saddle horse.

10. You can wash the girths if they are of the string or Cottage Craft variety. Make sure that they are dry before you use them again.

11. Webbing or lampwick can be brushed. Leather (not often used by ponies) must be cleaned after every ride.

12. Numnahs should be washed regularly — but **not** in detergents. It is very difficult to get them thoroughly rinsed and a pony's skin can become very sensitive to a detergent. Use soap flakes which have been well dissolved. Rinse very thoroughly. Spin dry or hang up to dry. Do not let numnahs get too dirty. They will rub the pony's back if you do not clean them regularly.

Lastly, don't forget that headcollars have to be cleaned as well, as must all other leather parts, rugs, rollers and New Zealand rug leg straps.

OWNING A PONY

Don't – until you have considerable experience in riding and horsemanagement.

Owning a pony is not a question of turning him out in a large field and letting him look after himself. Ponies need to be seen **at least** twice a day.

The type of pony

1. He should be quiet to handle, quiet when shod, quiet in a stable and quiet when out in traffic. He should also be easy to catch.

2. A Moorland or Native bred pony is best as a first pony. They are much more hardy and easier to keep than other breeds. **Never** have a thoroughbred-cross pony for your first one. They require much more care and demand considerable riding skill.

3. Always seek expert advice when you buy a pony. Always ask a veterinary surgeon to examine a pony and if possible arrange to have it on trial for a week.

4. Make sure that you have adequate grazing and shelter for any pony you buy, and can afford all the equipment you will need. **Buying** the pony is the cheapest part of owning him!

5. Age and height

Do not buy a young pony as your first one.
Young ponies need a great deal of care,
attention and knowledge. It is very easy to
spoil a pony if you ask too much from him.
The ideal age for a first pony is 9-10 years.
Buy a pony that will last you for two years.
You will be ready for a more advanced one
after this.

What a pony will need

A field

1. An area of about 1 − 1½ acres per pony is
   generally thought to be ideal. You should
   divide the field so that the pony is only
   using one half at a time; the other half will
   be resting. Doing this will always mean
   that you have fresh grazing for him. Grass
   does not grow if it is being walked on
   constantly!

2. **Fencing** − A good strong hedge is best, as
   it provides shelter and food as well as
   security. Ponies love eating young shoots in
   spring and autumn when they are
   changing their coats. A wall is also good,
   provided that it is high enough and strong
   enough to serve its purpose.

   Posts and rails can be secure and safe
   provided they are looked after, repaired
   and creosoted regularly. They can be a
   problem though if the ponies in the field
   chew the wood.

Straight wire and posts are **not** a good form of fencing, although they are considerably cheaper than the types mentioned above. Ponies may not see the wire and may gallop into it, though to make it show up, you can hang strands of blue plastic to help them see it.

Barbed wire should **not** be used. Ponies can get badly injured by barbed wire and when it is rusty, it breaks and can cause very serious cuts.

Electric fencing should only be used as a temporary fence and must have strips attached to it, so that the pony can see where it is. Electric fencing is rarely high enough to make a secure fence for a pony and it should really only be used in an emergency.

3. **A gate** − A good gate − metal if possible, and wide enough to get the pony through easily, is essential. If your gate is hanging by one hinge, with part of it missing, you won't keep your pony in his field. Your gate should also have a padlock on it, preferably one without a chain. There are a lot of people around who steal ponies and you must make it impossible for them to steal yours. Make sure too that the gate cannot be lifted off its hinges, and always remember that chains can be cut.

4. **Water** − The very best source of water for a pony is running water from a stream which is deep enough to be clean. It also needs to have a gravel bottom and easy

access for the pony. Streams like this rarely run dry in summer and they never freeze over in winter.

A water trough with a mains supply is good, **but**:

a. Remember that it must be cleaned regularly.

b. The pipe must be lagged to stop it freezing in winter.

c. The trough must be checked regularly to make sure that it is working properly.

All water troughs need to be raised off the ground or they will get damaged at the base. A trough should also have a hard surround, so that the pony does not have to plough through deep mud to get a drink.

Another source of water for your pony is an old bath with a removable plug, provided that you can fill it easily. Baths that you can drain are much easier to keep clean than ones that have to be emptied by hand. It is important to clean and refill water supplies like this two or three times a week.

REMEMBER: A PONY CANNOT LIVE WITHOUT WATER

5. **Shelter** − For a pony living on his own, a stable with the door hooked back will provide good shelter. When you need to keep him in, and during bad weather it will provide him with somewhere warm and dry. In summer, he will be able to wander in to take shelter from flies.

If you have more than one pony, a much larger shelter, with a completely open front, is much safer. Ponies can bully each other, and confined spaces can be

94

dangerous when a kicking match takes
place. Trees, hedges and walls will provide
adequate shelter for most ponies.

The type of shelter to avoid is the one with
a roof made from old, loose, flapping
sheets of corrugated iron. These leak, they
clatter and knock when the wind blows and
they frighten ponies more than they help
them.

Points to remember about your field

Never have trailing barbed wire, rubbish, broken bottles, or
anything on which a pony can injure himself lying in your
field. Be on the look-out for hazards like these when you are
out riding too!

Tack

Your pony will need:

A saddle, leathers/
irons, 2 pairs of girths,
2 numnahs

A bridle,
2 pairs of reins

A headcollar,
2 ropes

Grooming Kit
(in a box or bag)

Body brush, metal curry comb

Dandy brush

Hoofpick

Plastic/rubber curry comb

2 sponges – different types and colours

Stable rubber

(Chamois leather)

Water brush

Rugs

If your pony is in a stable, he must have a complete set of rugs.
(If he is out part of the time, he needs a New Zealand rug.)

Day rug

Night rug – jute

Roller – adequately padded

Sweat rug – like a string vest

New Zealand rug for cold and wet weather (if the pony is out all winter, you need 2 of these, so that one can be dried while he is wearing the other)

A sack (this is very useful for putting on a pony and drying him when he is dirty. To make a blanket out of a sack, undo the stitching of two hessian feed sacks. Spread them out and sew them together to make a big square. This will cover your pony from head to tail!

How to look after:-

THE FIELD

Pick up all the droppings on alternate days. This is very important. Ponies will not eat grass near their own dung. The grass becomes coarse and dark green. If the field is not cleaned, it will soon become horse-sick and will have to be rested. Harrowing the droppings just spreads the trouble. If your pony has worms, he will just keep reinfecting himself, if you do not pick up his droppings.

When you are resting one half of your field, it must be thoroughly cleaned, perhaps fertilized if the grass is poor, and then left for a few weeks. If the field is a reasonable size and has good fencing, cattle can be grazed to eat the patches the pony doesn't like. Cows will eat around horse dung and horses will eat around cow dung. Cows and ponies also eat in different way. Cows wrap their tongues around the grass and pull, whereas ponies nibble with their teeth. These different methods of eating grass encourages it to grow. If you don't have a cow of your own, try making friends with a farmer and ask to 'borrow' a cow! Once the grass has been eaten down a little, the cow can be returned and the pony can return to his second half.

This diagram shows a well thought out plan for a pony's field.

It is a good idea to build a long shelter, so that it serves **both** halves of the field. Put a partition down the middle to keep the pony in one half of the shelter when he is in field A and one half when he is in field B.

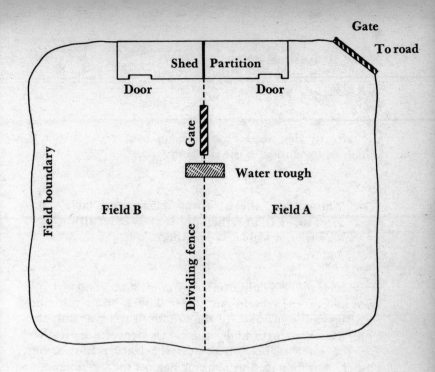

The water trough can also serve both fields.

The shaded areas are hard standing, so that
the pony can go for a drink and pass through
the gate without having to walk through a sea
of mud.

When laying out your field, it is important not
to create any narrow places where the pony
might get trapped. For this reason the shelter
should be built against the fence or out in the
field.

Ponies need company, even if the other pony or ponies are in
another field. Provided that they can be seen your pony will
be happy. Lonely ponies will try to push down fences and even
jump out in search of a companion.

How to look after:-

TACK

I've already described how to clean your tack, but it is important to store it in the right way too.

> **The golden rule is, always clean your tack after using it, and then put it away carefully.**
> This way, it will last a long time.

If you have to rest a saddle on the ground, stand it up with the knee rolls on the ground, **resting on a sack or a cloth**, and with the cantle, or back of the saddle, leaning against the stable. Put the girths under the cantle between the leather and the stable. This will protect the leather from being scratched or damaged by rubbing against the building.

> **Do not leave tack lying on the floor, it will get dirty and damaged.**

'A place for everything and everything in its place' is a good motto for the tack room. Stick to it and you will always be able to find your equipment.

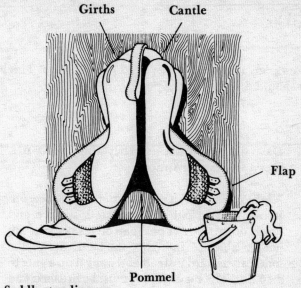

Girths   Cantle

Flap

Pommel

Saddle standing up
against a stable with
girths protecting the
cantle.

How to look after:-

GROOMING KIT

Keep everything neatly in a bag or box. A box is better as you
can see everything and it is easier to keep clean. If your
brushes are dirty, you won't be able to clean your pony. So,
wash all your brushes regularly and leave them to dry by
standing them on their sides. Be careful too not to leave them
standing too close to the heat. If you do, the wooden backing
will be damaged.

How to look after:-

RUGS

If your pony needs rugs, **they** need looking after. This is what you should do with each type.

Day rug — Brush it regularly when it is in use. Clean the leather straps.

Night rug — Wash this at the end of the season. It can be laid out on a concrete surface and hosed down. Do not put soap on it since you will not be able to rinse this out later. Scrub the soiled areas hard instead and hang it on a gate to drip dry. The blanket part must be brushed and repaired if it is damaged. Thoroughly clean and oil the straps before putting the rug away.

Roller — Regularly clean all the leather parts. Scrub all the soiled areas with cold water. Repair the edges of the webbing using button thread and a blanket stitch, if they begin to fray.

Sweat rug — Wash this as soon as it becomes dirty and hang it out to dry.

New Zealand rug — Do not allow this to remain damaged without patching it. If you get a tear, join the two sides with blanket stitching. Stitch the raw edges with double button thread and oversew the stitching. Repair the blanket underneath with wide tape. Clean all the leather parts. The leather used on outdoor rugs has been specially treated. It is called **chromed**

leather. This still needs to be cleaned in the usual way, but it must also be oiled when it is dry. This keeps it supple.

When your New Zealand rug is not in use, have any necessary repairs made at the saddlers. Put it on a concrete surface and hose it thoroughly until it is clean. Then hang it on a gate to dry. Once it is dry, lay it on a clean concrete surface and waterproof it with a tent proofer, which you can buy from any camping shop. The brand I use is called Fabsil. Paint the liquid onto the rug carefully, going over each seam twice. The proofer must be allowed to dry away from heat and it must not get wet until it has totally dried. We try to dry out treated rugs over a gate. They smell terrible if you dry them indoors and the fumes can be dangerous. You have to keep an eye on the weather, that's all!

New Zealand rugs should be proofed every year and then put away carefully. Fold them as little as possible.

LOOKING AFTER YOUR PONY DURING THE SEASONS

Spring

The grass is growing fast at this time and the pony should not be allowed out all the time on lush grass. He will get too fat and he may also get **Laminitis** or Foot Fever. This is a serious complaint which may permanently damage him. **Never** let a pony get too fat, it is unkind and unwise.

Your pony will be losing his winter coat in the spring and will need grooming every day to remove loose hair. He will try to rub off his coat on fences and his shelter, and he may even try to bite himself. If he consumes too much of his coat by biting at it, he may collect a lot of it in his stomach which will make him ill. It is very important that you remove it all for him. You'll find the plastic curry comb the most useful piece of kit. Collect all the loose hair and put it in your dustbin.

Ponies seem to need wood in the Spring and Autumn, when they are changing their coats. If you have a hedge in your field, your pony will nibble this and not your fences!

Alternatively, you can collect a small quantity of willow branches and tie these on the haynet ring for the pony to pull at. You will find that he will strip all the leaves and the bark.

Summer

Flies can be very troublesome at this time of the year and to avoid them your pony is probably better kept in during the day and turned out at night.

Make sure that he has enough water at all times. Keep an eye on the condition of the grass. If it starts to look burned by the wind and the sun, he may need to be moved into his other field.

If you see your pony cantering around and obviously worried, look at his legs when you next groom him. You will probably find that **gadflies** have been laying their bright yellow eggs all down his legs and over part of his body. These eggs must be removed, either with a **bot knife**, which you can get from your saddler, or by picking them off with your fingers. Your pony must not be allowed to bite them and swallow them. Eggs like these can cause internal damage to the pony's stomach. If you suspect that he has eaten some, ask your Pony Club, or veterinary surgeon for advice on worming.

If the flies are very bad around your pony's head, you can put on a headcollar with a fringe that keeps them out of his eyes at least.

Autumn

The pony will start to grow a new coat now and by late autumn you should not be grooming him with a body brush if he is living out. He needs to collect a layer of grease to keep himself warm and this is removed by constant grooming. Use the dandy brush to keep him clean.

Check the condition of the grass too. If this supply is running short, your pony may need supplementary hay.

Winter

To stay in good condition, your pony will need a New Zealand rug during winter. Small ponies are often better without a rug, but **the larger the pony the more protection it needs**.

106

A pony needs food to keep himself warm, and if he has no rugs, he will use this food for warmth and not for building up his energy. The result may be that he gets very thin if you do not give him enough protection, or if you are working him hard in the winter without giving him enough food.

Pay extra care and attention to his feet at this time of the year. If his field is muddy, he may pull off his shoes. Ponies left out in winter, in wet, muddy conditions, sometimes get cracks in their heels which become very sore and make the pony lame. So, if your pony is outside in the winter, inspect his heels and legs every day to make sure that he has not developed any sores.

When you put out hay for your pony, put it in a hayrack or net. If you have more than one pony in the field, put out a pile for each pony, plus a couple of extra piles. Ponies will bully each other and will chase other ponies off their piles if they think they have more to eat. By laying a couple of extra piles, you will be sure that all your ponies will have enough to eat. Space the piles out so that the ponies cannot kick each other while they are eating.

It is important to feed your pony regularly each day, at the same time. You would be bad tempered if your breakfast arrived an hour late, and so is your pony. With more than one pony the problem is greater and it is usually when their meals are late that ponies start crowding at gates and kicking each other.

Routine is very important for a pony. He plans his day around what he knows is going to happen. Ponies have 'clocks' in their tummies. If you are late with their meals, they will start to 'call' you. Similarly, they will lie down at a definite time and feed at a definite time. Upset a pony's routine and you can expect trouble. When you have to feed several ponies, take someone else with you, so that the ponies don't all crowd round **you**. Always feed the same pony first and they will soon learn the order in which you feed them.

Water is very important. If thick ice forms in a trough, a pony may not be able to break it to get a drink. Since hose pipes soon freeze in very cold weather, you may have to carry water to your pony in buckets. To avoid lasting damage, be sure that you have protected your pipes and taps before the very cold weather comes.

Provided that your pony is given plenty of hay, water and shelter, he will be all right in winter. Remember that snow is another matter. We find it difficult to adjust our eyes to the glare of snow in bright sunlight, even though we can wear dark glasses. For ponies the problem is far worse. In deep snow, you need to bring a pony inside to protect its eyes and also to keep him in good condition. He cannot find food in snow and the long, cold nights will make him lose condition quickly.

FEEDING

Feeding is an art, but here are some general rules. These apply to stabled ponies, but they may help you with a grass-kept one too.

1. **Feed little and often** − this makes it as near as you can to living in the open. A pony grazes and rests, grazes and rests. His stomach is small and he cannot take too much.

2. **Feed plenty of bulk** − hay when he can't get grass. He cannot digest his food unless he has enough of it.

3. **Feed according to the work your pony is going to do**. In summer he will need more concentrates (nuts and oats) because you will be riding him harder.

4. **Give him water BEFORE a hard feed**. He may have a little drink during or after a feed and this will not hurt him. A **big** drink will wash down some of his undigested food from his stomach and he may get colic.

5. A stabled pony **must** have something 'green' every day.

6. **Never work a pony immediately after a feed**. He must have at least 1-1½ hours before he works. The stomach is very near the lungs. If it is full, it will interfere with his breathing and may cause indigestion.

7. **Do not change the type of food you give your pony too suddenly** and do not introduce new food in too large a quantity. Start by giving ½ 1b (250 gm) of the new food and work up if necessary.

8. **Feed good quality, clean food**. Poor quality food will be bad for your pony.

9. **Keep the same feeding hours every day**.

10. **Water should be clean** and not just 'topped up'. If it is clean enough for you to drink, it will be clean enough for your pony!

11. **Whenever your pony is out of work, drop his hard feed and give him more hay.**

HANGING UP A HAYNET

The ring from which you hang a hay net should be high enough for you to just reach, but not as low as the **tying** or **wracking ring**.

Pass the drawstring of the net through the ring and pull the net up. Pass the drawstring through the **bottom** of the hay net and pull it upwards. Tie a quick release knot to secure it and **pass the end through**.

The net should be high enough — **when empty** — to prevent the pony from getting his feet in it. But it should not be **so** high that he has to reach up to it and so get seeds falling into his eyes.

If you do not pass the
ends of the drawstring
through the release-
knot loop, the pony
may pull it undone
and get tied up in the
loose net.

GENERAL CARE

Regular shoeing

Regular worming

Once a year the pony's teeth should be filed by a vet

Tetanus and flu injections are advisable

Care after a Prevac (flu) injection is vital. This is what you must do to avoid trouble. The pony should not be in hard work at the time of the injection. After the first injection, he must have **two weeks** without being ridden. He can be turned out and brought in at night, but do not ride him. During the next two weeks he may have gentle exercise, but there must no cantering, jumping or long rides. He then has his **second** injection and is out of work for − 10 − 14 days. After this you can start bringing him up quickly, but do not do any excessive work for at least 2 − 3 weeks. In 9 months to a year after these injections the pony will need a booster, after which he must be out of work for a week − 10 days.

Make sure that you have a vaccination certificate filled in by your vet. This goes everywhere with your pony if you are competing at big shows. Nearly all show secretaries need to see a photocopy of your certificate.

Tetanus injections do not put your pony out of action for quite so long. These are given at roughly the same intervals and a week's rest following each one is usually adequate.

COMPETITIONS AND ORGANIZATIONS

When you can ride well, there are many branches of equestrian competition which you can enjoy.

The most important organization for children is **The Pony Club**, which is part of **The British Horse Society**. You can find out how to join and what the Pony Club does for its members by writing to:

> **The Pony Club,**
> **British Horse Society,**
> **National Equestrian Centre,**
> **Stoneleigh,**
> **Warwickshire,**
> **CV8 2LR**

There are many branches of the Pony Club holding rallies, lectures, competitions, camps and other events. This will be your first introduction to competing on a pony and you will be able to take examinations as well.

The British Show Jumping Association is based at Stoneleigh as well. This is the governing body of the sport in the United Kingdom and it has a junior section that caters for young riders.

If you are interested in eventing, the Pony Club also runs events for its members.

If you are interested in long distance riding, the **Endurance Horse and Pony Society of Great Britain** are responsible for holding long distance rides all over the country. They hold Junior Classes with the Senior section and hold lectures and meetings from February to October. For further information on the EHPS write to me at:

**Long Distance Riding Centre,
Bourton-on-the-Water,
Gloucestershire.**

The British Horse Society also run long distance rides, but for riders over 17.

HUNTER TRIALS

Many riders who hunt during the autumn and winter enjoy entering their horses for cross-country competitions either at the beginning or the end of the hunting season. Hunter trials are the most common of these competitions.

A hunter trial tests a horse's speed and its ability to jump. Hunter trial courses are about 2.5 to 3 km long and contain jumps that a horse would expect to find in the course of a normal hunt — hedges, ditches, fences of various kinds and sometimes gates that the riders have to open and close.

Hunter trials are not designed or intended as competitions for selected horses. Horses that are regularly hunted will always perform well in hunter trials, provided that they are fit. Since hunter trials are held at either end of the hunting season, it is important that the horse entering trials at the beginning of the season (in the autumn) should begin his training a couple of months beforehand, to be fit in time. Horses taking part in spring hunter trials will have had a whole season of hunting to get fit and become used to jumping again. Here again it is important not to overwork the horse when he is hunting, so that he is too tired to go flat out round the hunter trial course.

Hunter trials are the most informal type of cross-country riding competition. They are well suited for preparing a horse for the hunting field and many horses and riders who have their eyes set on the demanding competition of three-day events, begin their careers in the local hunter trials.

TEAM CHASING

Team chasing is less than twenty years old, yet even in this short time it has become a very popular cross-country sport with both riders and spectators.

As its name suggests team chasing involves more than one rider. A team is made up of four riders, who ride round a jumping course of usually 3 to 5 km, with the time of the third rider to finish being taken as the team's score.

The jumps in team chases are a mixture of those found on a hunter trial course and some of the more difficult jumps usually found in the cross-country section of an eventing competition.

Successful team chase horses have to be able to gallop fast, but they also need to be able to jump very well. It's not unusual to find jumps on a team chase course that are higher than those on a three-day event course, though they are never as complicated. So there is no value in riding a horse that can gallop like a Derby winner, if it cannot jump the obstacles on the course.

Team chase horses often need to be able to gallop faster than eventers as well. They have to gallop round the course very fast and since courses often have thirty or more jumps, horses need to be very fit to compete successfully. As all four horses in a team ride together, no one horse can afford to be slower or less fit than the others. (In many team chase competitions, there is even one jump on the course which three horses in the team **have** to jump together. There is a judge at this fence who deducts seconds if the horses fail to jump together. So it is important that the horses in a team should be able to jump alongside others).

Team chases usually take place at the same time as hunter trials, in the autumn and early spring, to fit in with the hunting season. So the preparation of a team chase horse depends on when he will be competing.

POINT-TO-POINTS

The name 'point-to-point' racing suggests how this sport developed. Its other name 'steeplechasing' gives you an even clearer idea. In the eighteenth century members of local hunts would often race each other from one point to another, to prove whose horse was the faster. Frequently the points they raced from were from sight of one village steeple to another. As these races became more popular, the courses became more organized and the riders raced each other over a specially prepared circuit instead of riding across farmland, as they did in the hunting field. Even though point-to-point racing started as a cross-country event, today it looks more like the horse racing you see on the television.

It is still an amateur sport, however, and any rider may enter a point-to-point, provided that he or she meets the requirements of the hunt organising the meeting. (These usually involve hunting a certain number of times in the season and paying the hunt subscription).

Point-to-points are raced directly against other competitors, with all the horses galloping round the course at one time, instead of individually against the clock. The rules of point-to-points are laid down by the National Jockey Club, which controls horse racing in the United Kingdom, and a point-to-point race is conducted like a race at more formal, professional race meetings. The jockeys have to weigh in before a race; the horses are paraded before being mounted, so that the spectators can have a good look at them and decide which one to back with their money; and there is an unsaddling enclosure for the first four horses in the race, where the jockeys of these horses have to be weighed again. It is not surprising therefore that many racehorses start their racing careers running in point-to-points, where the competition is friendly and easier than professional race meetings.

The jumps on a point-to-point course stand about 1.3m high, so a point-to-point horse needs to be a good jumper. He also needs stamina, the energy to jump these fences at a gallop and race like this for about 4km.

SHOW JUMPING

When you think of the popularity of events like the Horse of the Year Show and the Royal International Horse Show, it's hard to believe that show jumping as we know it is less than forty years old.

Today there are large indoor arenas and specially built show jumping grounds all over the world devoted to the sport. Yet before the Second World War show jumping was only a minor sport enjoyed by a few enthusiasts. Its great popularity today owes a lot to television.

Show jumping is ideally suited to a television audience. The excitement and thrill of the riding, the colour and variety of the jumps and the success or failure of each horse and rider at every jump, which is easy to spot on television, make show jumping a sport that can be enjoyed by everyone – even those who have never sat on a horse in their lives.

Today show jumping competitions all over the world and at all levels, from small agricultural shows to the international competitions like the Nations Cup, are judged by the same set of rules. These have been laid down by the **Federation Equestre Internationale** (International Equestrian Federation), the governing body that controls the sport throughout the world.

Success or failure in a show jumping competition is judged by the success with which a horse and rider ride round a circuit and clear the jumps on that circuit. If a fence or part of a fence is knocked down, penalties are awarded. The horse and rider with the lowest number of penalties at the end of the competition is the winner.

Some of the most exciting show jumping competitions are those raced against the clock, when horses and riders try to complete the circuit in a faster time than the other competitors. In these competitions penalties are awarded in the form of time faults. There is no point in completing the circuit faster than anyone else, if you knock over most of the fences in the process and so collect a large number of time faults.

In some competitions, too, the jumps are made more difficult as rounds progress, so that one by one riders and horses are eliminated until the winner is left ahead of the rest of the field.

Although the obstacles on a show jumping circuit all look different, there are in fact two principal types - **high jumps** and **long jumps**. High jumps can be five-bar gates, walls, or oxers (a hedge set between two fences of parallel poles), for example. Long jumps, on the other hand, test a horse's skill at jumping at full stretch across an obstacle like a water jump, or a triple bar or staircase fence made from parallel poles rising in layers in the direction in which the horse must jump. As you might expect, the most difficult obstacles combine both height and breadth. The Hog's back is a jump with three sets of parallel poles in which the middle set stands higher than the two on either side. The temptation for a horse is to drop its hind legs after clearing the highest pole, and so knock off the ones on the far side.

Obstacles need not necessarily be individual fences. Some of the most demanding, and exciting to watch, are those which combine two or three fences set close together. A horse and rider have to pace these obstacles perfectly. They need to clear the first at just the right speed to fit in the few strides that are needed before taking off for the second and then the third. Fences that are less than 12m away from each other are judged as being part of the same obstacle. These combination fences, as they are called, are designed to test a horse's flexibility and include both high and long jumps close together.

The riders only have a quarter of an hour to examine a course before a competition gets underway. This time is very important. You will see the riders looking carefully at each fence to see how high it is, how it is made and how much of a

knock it will stand before part of it is knocked down. Riders also use this inspection time to pace out the approaches to the jumps so that they can judge how many paces their horses will need to get into their stride before jumping each fence cleanly. Correct pacing is vital when the horse is trying to complete the circuit as fast as possible. Walking the course also helps each rider to see the order in which the fences must be jumped. Jumping fences in the wrong order can lead to a disqualification, but if you have ever watched show jumping, you will know that the riders and horses have to criss-cross the arena with sharps turns and tight corners to move from one jump to the other.

At the top level of show jumping, there are often fifteen jumps on a circuit which will demand as many as eight changes of direction as well as full 'U' turns. Little wonder that modern show jumping is now big business with high prize money and high costs. Many of the world's leading show jumpers now receive sponsorship from industrial and commercial backers to help them cover the expenses of top competitions.

DRESSAGE

'Dressage' is a French term for the training of horses. Today it is used to describe a series of movements that test a horse's development and the state of his training.

Dressage is first and foremost an art. You could say that it started as soon as men began riding horses, thousands of years ago. They needed to develop the skills which made the horse go where they wanted it to go. Dressage, in the way that we understand and use the term today, really began in the sixteenth century. Famous riding schools were founded in Europe, where great attention was paid to training horses to perform elegant, complicated movements both on the ground and in the air. Horses were trained to move on their hind legs alone; they were taught to perform stylish leaps into the air; and they were taught to move at a walk, a trot and a canter under perfect control.

Modern competitive dressage follows similar lines. Competitions take place on many levels ranging from simple Pony Club tests to the highest levels of the Grand Prix and the Olympic Games. There is a special **Dressage Bureau** of the FEI which controls the sport.

The FEI gives the following definition:

'The object of dressage is the harmonious development of the physique and ability of the horse. As a result, it makes the horse calm, supple, and keen, thus achieving perfect understanding with its rider. These qualities are revealed by: the freedom and regularity of the paces; the harmony, lightness and ease of movements; the lightening of the forehand and the engagement of the hindquarters; the horse remaining absolutely straight in any movement along a straight line and bending accordingly when moving on curved lines. The horse thus gives the impression of doing of his own accord what is required of him.'

This means that the horse and rider need to have a perfect understanding of each other in order to perform dressage tests successfully.

Dressage tests begin with the horse and rider moving correctly at a walk, a trot and a canter, with a number of stops and starts. These three paces are tested from the Preliminary level of the Campaign school (called in French the **Basse-école**) through to the Grand Prix, the highest level of the High school, or **Haute-école**. As higher levels are reached, the variations in these paces become more and more difficult to perform smoothly and naturally.

In the **Haute-école** tests, horses are required to turn on their hindquarters; they have to change legs in their stride and have to move smoothly both forward and sideways. For the riders, this requires a total understanding of the way in which a horse moves, as well as a perfect seat and very well developed riding technique.

Dressage competitions are very formal occasions. They take place in rectangular, boarded areas, around which the judges sit. Each competitor has to move through a series of tests in a strict order and each test is marked by the judges as it performs. The marks given for each movement are as follows: O − Movement not performed; 1 − Very bad; 2 − Bad; 3 − Fairly bad; 4 − Insufficient; 5 − Sufficient; 6 − Satisfactory; 7 − Fairly good; 8 − Good; 9 − Very good; 10 − Excellent. The formality of the competition is carried into

the appearance of both horse and rider. Dressage horses must appear in the arena perfectly groomed and with immaculate tack. Riders usually wear tails and top hats, spotless breeches and beautifully polished high boots with spots.

LONG DISTANCE RIDING

Long distance riding is still a fairly new sport in Europe. In the USA, where it is called **trail riding**, it has been a popular event for horse lovers for longer.

Long distance riding obviously involves riding long distances, which might sound straightforward at first, but which is in fact a carefully controlled process of training a horse to cover distances of 30 to 160 km in 24 hours. For, in long distance riding, it is the horse's condition at the end of the ride, and not his place in the finishing order that decides the winner.

The great attraction of long distance riding to many horse owners is that the sport does not require a special type of horse. Horses with strong legs and feet, a good wide chest and an easy, smooth movement (with no tendency for the legs to brush together) should be able to take part in long distance competitions, provided that they are properly trained beforehand.

Long distance riding competitions take place over one, two or three days. Horses have to complete the course within a set average speed and the top awards go to those that do not collect any penalty points at the veterinary inspections along the route.

Because there is no element of racing, except in 'Endurance' classes, horses often do not move at anything faster than a trot, and the sport is looked on by many people as being a soft option — one that is undertaken by riders who don't have the guts to tackle eventing or hunting. Nothing could be further from the truth. Few things can be more uncomfortable than sitting in the saddle for hours on end in all weathers.

Long distance riders have to concentrate throughout the whole ride, particularly towards the end when their horses begin to get very tired and may make mistakes, unless the riders are quick to correct them. At the same time the rider has to think of the horse's condition, the whole time. He or she has to judge when the horse needs to ease up, or when they can afford to move faster to make up lost time. Long distance riding is demanding for both horse and rider. That's what makes it so appealing.

The best-known long distance ride in the United Kingdom is the **Golden Horseshoe Ride**, organized by the British Horse Society. This ride is held over two days and covers 120km across Exmoor. It is usually held at the beginning of May.

In the USA, probably the world's most famous long distance ride, the **Tevis Cup**, is held over 160km of rough country in California. Riders and horses in this event have to complete the course in 24 hours and those who do are presented with a gold and silver buckle showing one of the famous Pony Express riders.

The principal long distance competition in Australia takes place in the Blue Mountains in New South Wales. This is the **Quilty Ride**, which like the Tevis Cup, covers 160km. In South Africa the **National Endurance Ride** covers an even greater distance. Horses in this event have to cross over 200km of open country.

The key element in any long distance competition is the condition of the horse before, during and after the ride. This is why proper training is so important in the months leading up to the competition. The strains put on a horse are very great when it has to carry a rider along rough tracks, up steep hills, down the other and across uneven ground for kilometre after kilometre. The horse needs to be in excellent physical condition. It needs to be able to pick its own path through the terrain and it must remain comfortable throughout the ride. This last factor covers everything from the tack the horse is wearing to the way it walks and trots. Minor discomforts that might not cause too much trouble on an ordinary hack, can soon become serious after riding over rough country for six or seven hours.

Throughout a long distance ride there will be a number of inspection points where vets will check the condition of each horse before allowing it to continue on the next stage. A vet will check a horse's pulse and respiration rate at each inspection point as soon as it arrives. Half-an-hour later (longer towards the end of the ride) he will check these again, to see that they have returned to normal. If they are too high, this shows that the horse is not fully fit, and it will not be allowed to continue the ride.

Vets also check that horses are not dehydrating, losing too much body fluid. (Drinking regularly is very important on long distance rides. Several regular drinks are better for the horse than one long drink.) They will look at a horse's feet and legs to check for any signs of lameness and they will check the saddle too, making sure that this is not causing sores on the horse's back.

With such attention during the competition itself, it is important that long distance riders learn to carry out these checks themselves during training. Only by accurately measuring a horse's pulse and respiration can a rider know how the training is progressing and when the time has come to increase the distance covered and the strenuousness of the exercise.

For the successful long distance rider there is the satisfaction of winning a coveted award as well as the knowledge that he or she has achieved a real understanding with the horse, to bring it to this point of fitness when it can complete a very tough ride in better condition than any other competitor.

EVENTING

The FEI describes the three-day event as 'the most complete combined competition', but the same could be said of events that last one or two days. Eventing is a sport which tests the all-round ability of a horse and all events are divided into three distinct sections: dressage, show jumping and cross-country.

The order of these sections depends on the length of the event. In all events, the first test is always the dressage. In one and two-day events this is followed by the show-jumping. In three-day events the cross-country section comes after the dressage (and also after a speed and endurance test over roads-and-tracks and a steeplechase course) and the show jumping comes last. None of the three sections are as difficult as they would be in individual dressage, show-jumping, or hunter trial competitions, but following one after the other, they are a formidable challenge for any horse, and even the show jumping section of a three-day event, with jumps that are smaller than those found in a minor show jumping competition, is a great test for a horse that has been over a hard cross-country course only the day before.

Throughout any event, competitors are awarded penalty points for each section. At the end of the dressage section, the rider with the lowest score is the leader and further penalty points are added in the other two sections. The rider with the lowest score at the end of the event is the winner.

In the dressage test of an event competition the judges look first and foremost for obedience. They do not expect the horse to have reached the same standard as a 'pure' dressage horse, but they will be looking for straightness of entry; even, regular paces; correct cornering; and a ready acceptance of the bit.

In a three-day event the section after the dressage is an endurance test in which a horse rides round a roads-and-tracks circuit, goes round the steeplechase course and then rides round the roads-and-tracks circuit once more. This is followed by the most important part of the event, and the most exciting to watch, the cross-country.

Before competing in the cross-country section, all the competitors will have walked the course at least twice to look carefully at each of the obstacles and the approaches to them. The jumps will never be as high as those in a 'pure' show jumping competition, for example, but they are usually placed in very awkward jumping positions. They are also very solid and to a tired horse and rider they can look very menacing when approached from a difficult angle.

It takes a lot of nerve and absolute confidence to ride round the cross-country course. Penalties on this section are awarded for taking longer than the time allowed, and for refusing fences. If a horse refuses one fence three times, it is eliminated. You can also be eliminated for taking the wrong course, or for passing a boundary flag on the wrong side.

The purpose of the show-jumping section in a one or two-day event is to test that the horse is fit enough to take part in the cross-country that follows. Any horse which fails in the show jumping is not allowed to continue on to the cross-country. In a three-day event the show jumping section is designed to prove that a horse which has competed in the tough cross-country section and endurance tests of the previous day is still supple and has enough energy to take his rider obediently over the jumps. Easy as it may appear, this can often by a severe test for an eventer used to galloping over cross-country courses and very tired after a hard day's work.

The main three-day events are the World and European championships. In the United Kingdom, the **Badminton** and **Burghley** events are the principal competitions, while on the continent, the event held at **Luhmuhlen** in West Germany is one of the most important. In the USA, the **Ledyard** three-day event held in Boston holds the same importance as the European events mentioned.

POLO

It was during the nineteenth century that British army officers serving in India discovered a fast moving, exciting ball game played on horseback. They started playing this game themselves and, when it was brought back to the United Kingdom, it was called 'polo' after the Indian word 'pulu' — the root of the willow tree from which polo balls are still made in the East.

Polo is played between two teams of four (occasionally three) players mounted on horseback. The teams play on a polo pitch which is 275m long and 147m wide. At either end stand goal posts forming goals a little over 7m wide.

In a four-man polo team, the first two players (1 and 2) are forwards, or attacking players; the fourth player (4) is the back, who defends the goal; and the third player (3) is the mid-field player who links the other three.

The object of a game of polo is to score more goals than the other side. The game is divided into periods of play called **chukkas**. The length of each chukka depends on the standard of game being played, but most chukkas last for about 7½ minutes. The game is divided into these periods to allow the ponies to have a rest, since no animal, however fit it may be, can be expected to run about the field at a full gallop, turning sharply and competing with other horses for longer periods. In a polo game each player will ride at least two ponies to spread the work-load and avoid over-tiring his mounts.

Although the mounts used in polo are always called 'ponies', there is no longer any limit on their size. Any horse can be used in a game of polo, but experience has shown that horses over 16 hands are too unwieldy for the game.

A polo pony is a highly skilled animal. It has to be able to move from a stand into a gallop. It must be able to come to an abrupt stop and turn from a full gallop, and it needs to be able to ride in a straight line towards the ball when other ponies are galloping beside it and when its rider is swinging his stick very close to its head and feet. An experienced polo pony can often do much of the riding itself, leaving his master to concentrate on hitting the ball, which is difficult enough. Top-class ponies will sometimes see the ball before their riders and will take off after it, so there needs to be as much understanding between the polo pony and his rider as there is between the dressage horse and his rider, or the eventer and his rider. Little wonder then that the best polo ponies are very, very expensive.

Polo is a tough game. It is exhausting for the ponies and almost as tiring for the riders. The rules allow riders and ponies to 'ride-of' their opponents, which means that can try to push them off the line of the ball, to stop them hitting it.

For this reason both riders and ponies must wear protective garments. Ponies wear polo boots that protect the fetlock joints and the lower parts of their legs, in case their riders accidentally hit them or they get knocked by the hard wooden ball. The riders wear helmets made from cork, pith, or a hard synthetic material and knee-pads made of rubber or leather.

As well as these protective clothes polo players wear white riding breeches, brown leather top boots and the team shirt.

The great skill in playing polo lies in being able to control your pony while hitting the ball. Most players use their left hand to hold the pony's reins and carry their polo stick in the right hand. This stick is between 1.2 and 1.4mm long. There is a rubber or towelling grip at the top, attached to which is a sling. The shaft is made of cane about 19mm thick and the head is usually shaped like a cigar. This is also made of wood and is about 23cm long by 51mm in diameter at the centre.

There are four basic strokes in polo and the ball is always hit with the long side of the head. The principal strokes are: the **off-side forehander**; the **off-side backhander**; the **near-side forehander**; and the **near-side backhander**. There are variations of these which players learn as they become more skilled.

As with all ball and racket or stick games, the success of a polo shot lies in keeping your eye on the ball the whole time and this isn't easy when you're also riding a galloping pony and being pushed from one side by another player. Players have to lean down to hit the ball and this requires excellent balance. They also need to brace themselves for each shot and to do this a player will stand up in his stirrups and squeeze his kness into the pony to hold his body firm as he hits the ball. The secret of sending the ball a long way is not whacking it as hard as possible, but giving it a solid, controlled hit which is ideally timed with the pony starting to move just a little faster to give the ball extra momentum. So timing and positioning are essential for clean hits.

Above all, polo is a team game. Passing, intelligent positioning, backing up other team members and preventing your opponents from hitting the ball are important skills which every player has to learn. The best polo players give the impression that their mind is solely on the ball and that controlling the pony is something which is taking place automatically. While it may be instinctive, they still have to have absolute control of the pony and that means holding the reins in one hand and using knee pressure to guide it.

Today polo is played all over the world, though countries with a strong riding tradition naturally produce the best players and ponies. If any one country can be singled out as the leading polo nation it is probably Argentina which produces many outstanding players and which is the home of the world's most sought after ponies. Australia and the U.S.A. also produce many fine players. And among the British players, the Duke of Edinburgh and the Prince of Wales are two of the most accomplished.

CAREERS WITH HORSES

Working with horses is a 'way of life' rather than a well paid, 9 a.m. – 5 p.m. job. It involves working long hours, often in bad weather and having comparatively little time off. Set against this are plenty of advantages, the most obvious of which is that your are not tied to a desk and an office. You have the chance to ride good horses belonging to other people and **you** are responsible for their well-being and their happiness. You go to shows, events and sometimes to hunts. It is a responsible form of work with plenty of variety. You may even be lucky enough to work for famous people and look after famous horses.

All this needs **training**, if you are going to work your way to the top and earn a good wage. During your training, the work will be hard and the toughest test comes at the beginning. If you can put up with early training, you will find working with horses a very rewarding profession.

If your interest lies in teaching others to ride, there are three examinations you can take. These are set by the British Horse Society and are:-

Assistant Instructor (BHSAI)

Intermediate Instructor (BHSII)

Instructor (BHSI)

You can take the first when you are 17½ years old. This will require at least 3 months training, but a full year is much better as this will give you experience of a full year's routine in a stable.

Training to be a groom requires at least 18 months training. You can sit for your **Groom's Diploma** when you are 18, but it is better to take this when you are older and have greater experience of the work. This is a very advanced examination which lasts two days, but it qualifies you to run yards on any size, housing competition horses and possibly some hunters. The Groom's Diploma is set and awarded by the Association of British Riding Schools.

Either of these qualifications will enable you to find a job in this country or abroad.

If stud work appeals to you, get in contact with the **National Pony Society**, who are responsible for this work. You will need to train at a recognized stud and can later take two exams.

Train for the exam of your choice, go out and gain experience and you will find that working with horses is a worthwhile occupation.

Agricultural colleges now run **Horse Management** courses which cover all aspects of horse care, together with pasture management, book keeping and accounts. This is a useful course if you want to work in farm management and run a stud of your own.

Veterinary nursing appeals to some people, but unless you are going to join an Equine Practice, you will not have a lot of contact with horses. Most veterinary nursing is concerned with small animals.

Farriery is mainly a man's profession, but there are several girl farriers. It is a tough job and you need to be strong.

It doesn't really matter what aspect of working with horses you decide to follow as long as you **TRAIN** for that particular occupation. So many people apply to work as grooms without really thinking what the work involves and then become disappointed when they can only get the mucking out jobs. If you are good at your job and take a keen interest in your horses and ponies, you will find great satisfaction in what you do.

Have fun and make sure your pony does too!

FAMOUS RIDERS

David Broome

David Broome is one of
the most well known
and successful British
show jumping riders.
He holds the record for
winning the King
George V Gold Cup (5
times) and in 1970 he
became the first
British rider to win the
men's world
championship title.

David Broome first rode for his country in 1959.
In those days his horse was Wildfire. His next
successful horse, Sunslave, helped him to win an
individual bronze medal in the Olympic Games
held in Rome in 1960. In 1961 he and Sunslave
won the men's European championship. Then
in 1966 he teamed up with his most famous
horse, Mr. Softee, and together they won the
European championship again in 1967 and
1969 and another Olympic bronze in 1968. Two
years later David Broome became world
champion riding Beethoven, and since then
he has been at the forefront of British show
jumping.

Piero D'Inzeo

Piero is the elder of the two famous Italian show jumping brothers. His riding career started in the army and in 1949 he represented Italy for the first time in both the Olympic show jumping and three-day events.

Since then he has collected an impressive score of medals: four Olympic team medals, one European championship medal and two runner-up medals. His famous horses have been Uruguay, The Rock and Pioneer.

Raimondo D'Inzeo

Like his brother, Piero, Raimondo D'Inzeo rose to fame in the Italian cavalry. He first rode in the Olympics in 1952. He has won the same team medals as his brother, though he has also collected an individual gold medal, won on Posillipo in 1960 and an individual silver which he won on Merano four years earlier. In the same year he became world champion for the first time, also riding Merano, and four years later he won the world championship for a second time riding Gowran Girl. Apart from the German rider, Hans-Günter Winkler, Raimondo D'Inzeo is the only man to have won the world show jumping championship twice.

Pierre Jonquéres D'Oriola

In the 1950's and 1960's, this famous French rider was the world's leading competitor in show jumping competitions.

He is the only man to have won two individual Olympic gold medals, in 1952 and 1964, in the first case he had only ridden Ali Baba, an ex-polo pony, three times! Even so he walked off the top award. In 1966 D'Oriola became world champion riding Pomone.

Richard Meade

Richard Meade is a highly successful British three-day event rider.

In 1968 he won an Olympic gold medal as part of the British team and four years later he won two further gold medals, on team and one individual, riding Laurieston. Poacher was another of his very successful horses. Together they won the Badminton Three-Day Event in 1970 and later that year they helped the British team win the world championship event. Richard Meade is the only British rider to win three Olympic gold medals.

Captain Mark Phillips

Mark Phillips and Great Ovation won the Badminton Three-Day Event two years running in 1971 and 1972. In 1974 he won it again, this time riding the Queen's horse Columbus and in 1981 he won it a record fourth time on Lincoln.

He also competed in the British world championship team which won the title in 1970. A year later he was in the successful European championship team and in 1972 he won an Olympic gold medal, again in the British team.

Ann Moore

The story of Ann Moore and Psalm was one of the most successful in the late 1960's and 1970's. Ann trained the horse herself and together they took the show jumping world by storm.

In 1968 they won the European junior championship. In 1971 and 1973 they won two women's European championships and in 1972 they won an individual silver medal at the Olympics. Ann Moore and Psalm also won the Queen Elizabeth II Cup two years running in 1972 and 1973, when she shared it with Alison Dawes.

145

Hans Günter Winkler

Hans Günter Winkler
is West Germany's top
show jumping rider.
He rode for Germany
in 1956, 1960 and 1964
when the team won the
Olympic gold medal
three times.

He was world champion in 1954 and 1955. He won an individual gold medal in the 1956 Olympics riding his famous mare, Halla. In 1972 he won a fifth Olympic gold on Trophy. This gives him the greatest number of Olympic gold medals won by any rider.

Alwin Schokemohle

Alwin Schokemohle is another of West Germany's top show jumping riders.

In 1960 he helped Germany ride to success in the Olympic games, on Ferdl. Eight years later, riding Donald Rex he had the best individual score and helped Germany win a bronze medal. In 1976 he obtained the lowest score ever recorded by a winner in the Olympics — no faults. He shares this honour with Czech rider Frantisek Ventura. In 1975 he won the King George V Gold Cup on Rex the Robber. And ten years earlier he set a new German high jump record when he and Exakt cleared a fence 2.25m high!

Lucinda Prior-Palmer Green

Among British event riders, Lucinda Prior-Palmer Green is the most successful lady rider. She holds the ladies' record for winning the Badminton Three-Day Event in which she has come first four times. (She shares this record with Captain Mark Phillips).

In 1973 she won Badminton on Be Fair. In 1976 she won it on Wide Awake. In 1977 she won it on George. And two years later she won it again on Killaire. Lucinda was only 19 when she and Be Fair won Badminton for the first time. Two years later they became Individual European Champions and in 1977 Lucinda became the first rider to have won the European Championship twice and to have won the Badminton and Burghley events in the same year.

Pat Smythe

In the 1950's and early 1960's, Pat Smythe was the most successful international lady show jumping rider.

She was four times European women's champion in 1957, 1961, 1962 and 1963 — all gained on Flanagan. She also rode Flanagan in the Olympic Games in 1956 when women were allowed to compete for the first time. They helped the British team win the bronze.

USEFUL ADDRESSES

United Kingdom: The Pony Club,
British Horse Society,
National Equestrian Centre,
Stoneleigh,
Warwickshire,
CV8 2LR

Australia Equestrian Federation of Australia,
Royal Show Ground,
Epsom Road,
Ascot Vale,
3032,
Australia

Canada Canadian Equestrian Federation,
333 River Road,
Ottawa,
Ontario,
K1L 8B9
Canada

Eire: Equestrian Federation of Ireland,
58 Upper Leeson Street,
Dublin 4,
Eire

New Zealand: The New Zealand Horse Society,
P.O. Box 1046,
Hastings,
New Zealand

U.S.A. American Horseshows Association,
598 Madison Avenue,
New York,
New York,
10022,
U.S.A.

YOU CAN PLAY FOOTBALL *with* Gordon Banks
Illust. Mike Miller

Enjoy the exhilarating sport of football with World Cup
winner and goal keeper, Gordon Banks.

As a handbook for learning this fast-moving game from
scratch, or as an aid to improving technique, ploys and
performance, YOU CAN PLAY FOOTBALL will take you
through every aspect of the sport – development of the
game, rules and regulations, skilful manipulation of the
ball, team tactics and plenty of exercises, tips and advice
from one of the greatest and most respected figures in the
world of football.

0 552 54200 8   85p

YOU CAN SWIM *with* David Haller

Take a plunge into the dynamic sport of swimming with David Haller, former British team coach, and captain and competitor in the 1976 and 1980 Olympic games.

Whether learning to swim or improving your technique, whether you wish to swim for pleasure, competition or just survival, this comprehensive handbook takes you through gaining confidence in the water, developing the strokes, diving and fast, effective swimming for competitive racing, and includes games, exercises and advice from a great swimmer and top professional coach.

0 552 54197 4   95p

YOU CAN BE A GYMNAST *with* Avril Lennox
Illust. Mike Miller

Join the thrilling world of modern gymnastics with Avril
Lennox, MBE, former British Gymnastics Champion and
now coach to the British Gymnastics Team.

Whether you wish to make a start or improve your performance in the gymnastics' arena, you'll find everything you
need to know in this superb handbook. First-rate
information on how to begin, exercises for strength and
flexibility, elementary work on the floor and apparatus,
simple floor routines and plenty of tips and sound advice
from an experienced gymnast at the very top of her field.

0 552 54198 5   **£1.25**

YOU CAN PLAY CRICKET *with* Ted Dexter
Illust. Mike Miller

Experience all the excitement and tension of cricket with Ted Dexter, former Test player and Captain of England.

If you wish to learn this fascinating sport or simply want to improve your skills, then this is the book for you. How the match is played, rules and regulations, fielding, batting and bowling techniques and tactics, games and exercises to develop control and fluidity, and personal tips and hints for getting the most out of your game from an outstanding figure in the cricketing world.

0 552 54199 0   85p

CHALLENGE
by Gyles Brandreth; illust. Peter Stevenson

Can YOU eat a bowl of soup with a fork?
Can YOU blow a bubble to beat the world bubble gum record?
Can YOU put on every single pair of socks you own – one after the other?
Can YOU do up your buttons, peel a banana and comb your hair without using your thumbs?

Challenges for journeys, challenges for rainy days, challenges alone and challenges with friends – treasure hunts, brain busters, puzzles, tricks and daredevil dares – can you take a CHALLENGE?

0 552 54194 X   85p

FUN WITH PAINTS AND PAPER
100 Different Things to Do!
by Angela McGlashon; illust. Gillian Hurry

Paints, prints, patterns and pictures from Sponge Scapes to Starbursts and Marbellous Marbelling...

Decorations for all occasions – chains, murals, mobiles and friezes from Devil's Masks to Wrought Paper Medallions...

Cards and gifts for special people, from a fat string Mouse to Mouthwatering Mats – from Ping Pong Puppets to Japanese Kites...

Games to play and momentous magic from fairground fun to codes and treasure quests...

A dazzling century of things to do!

0 552 54190 7   85p

CRAZY DAYS
by Gyles Brandreth; illust. Peter Stevenson

BUDGIE DAY IN Cedar Rapids, U.S.A., 13th January

HIPPO DAY 25th May 1850 – The first hippo arrived in Great Britain

A COLD DAY FOR PEAS 6th March 1930 when frozen foods first appeared in the shops

BALLOON BURSTING DAY 19th July

Make a date with CRAZY DAYS for festive feasts, birthday beanos, anniversaries, jokes and riddles, tongue-twisters and astounding facts to celebrate the whole year through!

What's today's crazy day...?

0 552 54191 5   85p

SHADOW SHOWS
by Gyles Brandreth; illust. David Farris

Create a tremendous shadow spectacular with thrilling hand shadow techniques, puppets to make, prehistoric monster creations, mysterious magic and illusions, shadow plays and pantomines, and shadow characters to amaze and delight your audience.

Stage and screen settings, lighting, scripts, special effects, props and all the tricks of the trade are included in this superb shadow extravaganza – so dim the lights and let the show begin...

0 552 54192 3   85p

MAKING MODEL RACING CARS
written and illustrated *by* Peter Fairhurst

Re-create the dazzling world of the Grand Prix circuit with eight great champions representing the famous names of Formula 1 – Tyrell, Ferrari, Williams, McClaren, and the pre-war pioneers of racing, including Mercedes, Alfa Romeo, Benz and ERA.

These sleek, streamlined models, the most advanced and successful of their day, are simply constructed from card and balsa wood with the aid of first-rate diagrams and plans – each to perfect scale and with complete instructions for finishing and detail.

0 552 54197 4

85p

If you would like to receive a newsletter telling you about our new children's books, fill in the coupon with your name and address and send it to:

Gillian Osband,

Transworld Publishers Ltd,

Century House,

61–63 Uxbridge Road, Ealing,

London, W5 5SA

_____

Name ....

Address ....

....

CHILDREN'S NEWSLETTER

All the books on the previous pages are available at your bookshop or can be ordered direct from Transworld Publishers Ltd., Cash Sales Dept. P.O. Box 11, Falmouth, Cornwall.

Please send full name and address together with cheque or postal order—no currency, and allow 45p per book to cover postage and packing (plus 20p each for additional copies).